LinkedIn Marketing 2024

A Comprehensive Guide to Successful Marketing, Engagement, and Conversions with Proven Tactics, Techniques, and Strategies on the World's Largest Professional Networking Platform

Heinrich Brevis

Table of Contents

Introduction

In the rapidly evolving landscape of digital marketing, LinkedIn stands out as the premier platform for professionals seeking to establish meaningful connections, enhance their brand, and drive business growth. With over 700 million users spanning diverse industries and geographies, LinkedIn offers unparalleled opportunities for marketers to engage with a highly targeted and influential audience.

"LinkedIn Marketing 2024: A Comprehensive Guide to Successful Marketing, Engagement, and Conversions with Proven Tactics, Techniques, and Strategies on the World's Largest Professional Networking Platform" is your essential companion for navigating this dynamic environment. Whether you're a seasoned marketer looking to refine your approach or a newcomer eager to harness the power of LinkedIn, this book provides the insights and tools you need to succeed.

Why LinkedIn Matters

LinkedIn is not just another social media platform; it's a professional networking powerhouse where business leaders, decision-makers, and industry experts converge. Unlike other platforms that prioritize entertainment and casual interactions, LinkedIn is designed for professional growth, knowledge sharing, and business development. This unique focus makes it an ideal venue for B2B marketing, thought leadership, and high-value networking.

With LinkedIn, you can:

- **Build a Robust Professional Network**: Connect with industry leaders, potential clients, and like-minded professionals.
- **Enhance Your Brand**: Position yourself and your company as thought leaders in your field.
- **Generate Leads and Drive Sales**: Utilize sophisticated targeting options to reach your ideal audience.
- **Engage with Content**: Share articles, videos, and updates to foster engagement and discussion.

What This Book Offers

This guide is structured to provide a thorough understanding of LinkedIn marketing, from the basics to advanced strategies. It covers:

- **Getting Started**: Learn the fundamentals of creating a compelling LinkedIn profile and company page that attract attention and convey credibility.
- **Content Creation and Curation**: Discover how to craft content that resonates with your audience, from blog posts and articles to videos and infographics.
- **Engagement Strategies**: Explore techniques to increase interaction with your posts, join and participate in relevant groups, and use LinkedIn's messaging system effectively.
- **Advertising on LinkedIn**: Gain insights into LinkedIn's advertising options, including Sponsored Content, Sponsored email, and Dynamic Ads, and learn how to create campaigns that convert.

- **Analytics and Optimization**: Understand how to measure the success of your LinkedIn efforts using analytics tools and data-driven strategies to optimize your performance.

Proven Tactics and Real-World Examples

Throughout the book, you'll find proven tactics and real-world examples from successful LinkedIn marketers. These case studies illustrate how businesses and individuals have leveraged LinkedIn to achieve remarkable results. By studying these examples, you can adapt and apply similar strategies to your own LinkedIn marketing efforts.

Moving Forward with Confidence

LinkedIn is continually evolving, with new features and updates that enhance its capabilities and user experience. Staying informed and adaptable is crucial to maintaining a competitive edge. This book not only provides a comprehensive guide to current best practices but also encourages a mindset of continuous learning and adaptation.

As you embark on your LinkedIn marketing journey, remember that success on this platform requires a blend of strategy, creativity, and persistence. Whether your goal is to build a personal brand, generate leads, or drive business growth, LinkedIn offers the tools and opportunities to achieve it.

Welcome to "LinkedIn Marketing: A Comprehensive Guide to Successful Marketing, Engagement, and Conversions." Let's unlock the full potential of the world's largest professional networking platform together.

Chapter 1: Introduction to LinkedIn Marketing

In the realm of digital marketing, few platforms offer the targeted reach and professional engagement opportunities that LinkedIn does. As the world's largest professional networking site, LinkedIn has become an indispensable tool for businesses, marketers, and professionals aiming to establish a robust online presence, connect with industry leaders, and drive significant business results.

The Unique Power of LinkedIn

LinkedIn is a platform like no other. While other social media networks like Facebook, Twitter, and Instagram are often centered on personal sharing and entertainment, LinkedIn is uniquely focused on the professional sphere. This makes it an ideal venue for B2B marketing, professional networking, and career development.

Key features that set LinkedIn apart include:

- **Professional Focus**: Users come to LinkedIn to share professional achievements, industry news, and career updates, making it a fertile ground for serious business discussions and networking.
- **High-Quality Connections**: LinkedIn's network comprises influential professionals, including CEOs, managers, and decision-makers, offering valuable opportunities for meaningful connections.

- **Content Sharing**: LinkedIn allows users to publish articles, share updates, and post multimedia content that can enhance their professional brand and foster engagement with a targeted audience.
- **Job Opportunities**: With its extensive job listings and company pages, LinkedIn serves as a vital resource for both job seekers and recruiters.

The Evolution of LinkedIn Marketing

Since its launch in 2003, LinkedIn has continuously evolved to become a powerhouse for marketing and business development. Initially, it was a platform for job seekers and recruiters. However, recognizing the potential for business growth, LinkedIn expanded its features to support marketing efforts, including:

- **Company Pages**: Businesses can create dedicated pages to showcase their brand, products, services, and updates, building a professional online presence.
- **LinkedIn Ads**: With options like Sponsored Content, Sponsored InMail, and Dynamic Ads, LinkedIn provides robust advertising solutions to reach targeted professional audiences.
- **Sales Navigator**: This premium tool allows sales professionals to identify leads, build relationships, and manage their sales pipeline directly within LinkedIn.
- **Analytics**: LinkedIn offers comprehensive analytics tools to measure the effectiveness of marketing campaigns and profile performance, enabling data-driven decision-making.

Why LinkedIn Marketing Matters

In today's competitive market, having a strategic presence on LinkedIn is not just advantageous—it's essential. Here are several reasons why LinkedIn marketing should be a cornerstone of your digital strategy:

- **Targeted Reach**: LinkedIn's advanced targeting options allow you to reach specific demographics, industries, and job roles, ensuring your message gets in front of the right people.
- **Lead Generation**: LinkedIn is a proven platform for generating high-quality leads, particularly in the B2B sector, where connections can translate into significant business opportunities.
- **Brand Authority**: By sharing valuable content and engaging with your network, you can establish yourself and your business as industry leaders and build trust with your audience.
- **Networking Opportunities**: LinkedIn provides unparalleled opportunities to connect with potential clients, partners, and influencers who can drive your business forward.
- **Recruitment and Talent Acquisition**: LinkedIn is an invaluable tool for finding and attracting top talent, helping you build a strong and capable team.

Setting the Stage for Success

As you embark on your LinkedIn marketing journey, it's crucial to understand that success on this platform requires a blend of strategic planning, consistent execution, and continuous optimization. This book will guide you through each step of the process, from setting up your profile and company page to creating engaging content, running effective ad campaigns, and measuring your results.

Goals and Objectives

To make the most of LinkedIn marketing, start by defining clear goals and objectives. These could include:

- Increasing brand awareness
- Generating high-quality leads
- Building a network of industry contacts
- Establishing thought leadership
- Driving traffic to your website or landing pages
- Recruiting top talent

With these goals in mind, you can tailor your LinkedIn strategy to achieve measurable outcomes.

Leveraging LinkedIn's Features

Throughout this book, we will delve into the various features and tools LinkedIn offers to maximize your marketing efforts. From optimizing your profile and company page to leveraging LinkedIn Groups and utilizing advanced search capabilities, you'll gain a comprehensive understanding of how to make LinkedIn work for you.

In the following chapters, we'll explore:

- Creating a standout LinkedIn profile and company page
- Developing a content strategy that resonates with your audience
- Engaging with your network and building meaningful relationships
- Utilizing LinkedIn's advertising options for maximum impact
- Measuring success and refining your approach based on analytics

By the end of this book, you'll be equipped with the knowledge and skills to harness the full potential of LinkedIn marketing, driving engagement, conversions, and growth for your business.

Welcome to the world of LinkedIn marketing. Let's get started on building a powerful presence on the world's largest professional networking platform.

1.1 Understanding LinkedIn as a Marketing Platform

To fully harness the power of LinkedIn for marketing, it is essential to understand the platform's unique characteristics, features, and user demographics. LinkedIn is not just a social media network; it is a sophisticated ecosystem designed to foster professional relationships, knowledge sharing, and business growth.

The Professional Ecosystem

LinkedIn's core user base consists of professionals from various industries, including senior-level executives, managers, entrepreneurs, and entry-level employees. This diverse and influential audience makes LinkedIn an ideal platform for B2B marketing and professional networking. The platform is built around several key elements that support its professional focus:

- **Profiles**: Individual profiles serve as digital resumes, showcasing users' work experience, skills, education, and professional accomplishments. A well-crafted profile can significantly enhance personal branding and visibility.
- **Company Pages**: Businesses can create and manage company pages to highlight their brand, products, services, and corporate culture. These pages are crucial for engaging with followers and building a brand presence on LinkedIn.
- **Content Sharing**: LinkedIn enables users and companies to share a wide range of content, including articles, updates, images, and videos. This content can help establish thought leadership, drive engagement, and promote products or services.

Key Features for Marketers

LinkedIn offers a suite of features specifically designed to help marketers reach and engage their target audience. Understanding these features is the first step in crafting a successful LinkedIn marketing strategy:

- **LinkedIn Ads**: LinkedIn provides robust advertising options that allow marketers to create targeted campaigns. These include Sponsored Content, Sponsored InMail, Text Ads, and Dynamic

Ads. Each ad type has its unique benefits and can be tailored to specific marketing goals.

- **LinkedIn Groups**: Groups are communities of professionals with shared interests or industry affiliations. Participating in relevant groups can enhance visibility, facilitate networking, and position you as a thought leader.
- **Sales Navigator**: This premium tool is designed for sales professionals to identify potential leads, track prospects, and build relationships. It provides advanced search capabilities and leads recommendations based on your preferences.
- **LinkedIn Learning**: Offering a vast library of courses, LinkedIn Learning can be a valuable resource for continuous professional development and staying updated with the latest marketing trends and strategies.

Audience Insights

One of LinkedIn's most powerful features is its ability to provide detailed audience insights. LinkedIn's analytics tools allow you to understand your audience's demographics, engagement patterns, and content preferences. These insights can inform your marketing strategy, ensuring that your content and campaigns resonate with your target audience.

- **Demographic Data**: LinkedIn provides detailed demographic information about your followers and page visitors, including their job titles, industries, and locations. This data helps tailor your content to meet the specific needs and interests of your audience.
- **Engagement Metrics**: Track how users interact with your content through metrics such as likes, comments, shares, and click-through

rates. Understanding these metrics can help you identify what types of content perform best and adjust your strategy accordingly.

- **Campaign Performance**: For LinkedIn Ads, detailed performance reports show how your campaigns are performing in terms of impressions, clicks, conversions, and ROI. These insights are crucial for optimizing your ad spend and improving campaign effectiveness.

Competitive Advantage

LinkedIn's professional focus provides several competitive advantages for marketers:

- **Credibility and Trust**: LinkedIn's emphasis on professional connections and content means that users are generally more receptive to business-related messaging. This environment fosters credibility and trust, making it easier to build relationships and influence decision-makers.
- **High-Quality Leads**: LinkedIn's advanced targeting options allow you to reach specific audiences based on their job titles, industries, company sizes, and other criteria. This precision targeting ensures that your message reaches high-quality leads who are more likely to convert.
- **Thought Leadership**: Sharing insightful content and engaging in meaningful conversations can establish you and your business as industry leaders. This thought leadership can enhance your brand's reputation and attract a loyal following.

Leveraging LinkedIn for Different Marketing Goals

LinkedIn can support a variety of marketing objectives, from brand awareness to lead generation and customer retention. Here are some ways to leverage LinkedIn for different marketing goals:

- **Brand Awareness**: Use LinkedIn Ads and engaging content to increase the visibility and awareness of your brand among a targeted professional audience.
- **Lead Generation**: Utilize LinkedIn's advanced search and advertising tools to identify and connect with potential leads. Offering valuable content, such as whitepapers or webinars, can attract and capture leads.
- **Customer Engagement**: Keep your audience engaged with regular updates, industry news, and interactive content. Responding to comments and participating in discussions can foster a sense of community and loyalty.
- **Recruitment**: Promote job openings and showcase your company culture to attract top talent. LinkedIn's job posting and recruiter tools can streamline the hiring process and connect you with qualified candidates.

Understanding LinkedIn as a marketing platform is the first step toward leveraging its full potential. With its professional focus, robust features, and detailed audience insights, LinkedIn offers unique opportunities for marketers to connect with a high-quality audience, build brand authority, and drive business growth. As we delve deeper into the specific tactics and strategies in the following chapters, you'll gain the knowledge and tools to create a successful LinkedIn marketing plan tailored to your goals.

1.2 The Importance of LinkedIn in B2B and B2C Marketing

LinkedIn's distinctive professional environment makes it a powerful tool for both B2B (business-to-business) and B2C (business-to-consumer) marketing. While LinkedIn is often associated with B2B marketing due to its professional user base, it also offers significant opportunities for B2C marketers to connect with an audience that values professional development and business insights. Understanding how LinkedIn serves both B2B and B2C marketing can help you maximize its potential for your specific needs.

LinkedIn in B2B Marketing

LinkedIn is particularly well-suited for B2B marketing for several reasons:

- **Targeted Audience**: LinkedIn allows B2B marketers to reach decision-makers and influencers within companies. With advanced targeting options based on job title, industry, company size, and more, you can ensure your content and ads reach the right people.
- **Professional Context**: The platform's professional environment means that users are more receptive to business-related content, making it easier to engage them with industry insights, product information, and case studies.
- **Lead Generation**: LinkedIn provides tools like Sales Navigator and LinkedIn Ads to identify and connect with potential leads. These tools enable marketers to nurture relationships and move prospects through the sales funnel.

- **Thought Leadership**: By sharing valuable content and participating in industry discussions, B2B companies can position themselves as thought leaders. This enhances credibility and trust, which are crucial for building long-term business relationships.
- **Networking Opportunities**: LinkedIn's focus on professional connections provides numerous opportunities for networking with potential partners, clients, and collaborators. This can lead to strategic alliances and business growth.

Strategies for B2B Marketing on LinkedIn

- **Content Marketing**: Publish articles, whitepapers, and case studies that address industry challenges and offer solutions. This content can attract and engage decision-makers.
- **Webinars and Events**: Promote and host webinars or virtual events on LinkedIn to demonstrate expertise and engage with your audience in real time.
- **LinkedIn Groups**: Join and participate in groups related to your industry. Sharing insights and starting discussions can increase your visibility and establish your authority.
- **Personal Branding**: Encourage your employees, especially executives, to build and maintain active LinkedIn profiles. Their professional presence can enhance your company's brand and credibility.

LinkedIn in B2C Marketing

While LinkedIn is often associated with B2B marketing, it also offers valuable opportunities for B2C marketers:

- **Affluent Audience**: LinkedIn's user base tends to be more affluent and educated, which can be advantageous for B2C marketers targeting premium products or services.
- **Professional Insights**: Many LinkedIn users are interested in content that helps them advance their careers or businesses. B2C companies offering educational content, professional development tools, or business-related services can effectively engage this audience.
- **Brand Awareness**: LinkedIn can be a powerful platform for building brand awareness among professionals who value quality and innovation. Sharing stories about your brand, product launches, and customer success stories can resonate with this audience.
- **Employee Advocacy**: Encourage your employees to share company content and their experiences. This can amplify your reach and humanize your brand, making it more relatable to consumers.

Strategies for B2C Marketing on LinkedIn

- **Educational Content**: Share articles, videos, and infographics that provide value to your audience. This could include tips for career advancement, productivity hacks, or industry trends.
- **Customer Stories**: Highlight testimonials and case studies from customers who have benefited from your products or services. Personal stories can create an emotional connection and build trust.
- **Influencer Partnerships**: Collaborate with influencers who have a strong presence on LinkedIn. Their endorsement can lend credibility to your brand and expand your reach.

- **Targeted Advertising**: Use LinkedIn Ads to target specific demographics, such as job titles, industries, and interests. Tailor your messaging to resonate with the professional aspirations and needs of your audience.

The Overlap between B2B and B2C Marketing on LinkedIn

While B2B and B2C marketing strategies on LinkedIn have distinct differences, there are also areas of overlap that can benefit both types of marketers:

- **Content Marketing**: Both B2B and B2C marketers can leverage content marketing to provide value, build relationships, and drive engagement. The key is to tailor the content to the interests and needs of your target audience.
- **Engagement**: Active participation in groups, commenting on posts, and starting discussions can enhance visibility and foster connections, regardless of whether your focus is B2B or B2C.
- **Brand Building**: Consistent and strategic use of LinkedIn helps build a strong brand presence. Sharing your company's mission, values, and success stories can attract both business clients and consumers.
- **Employee Advocacy**: Empowering employees to act as brand ambassadors can extend your reach and build trust. Authentic employee stories and endorsements can resonate with a wide audience.

LinkedIn is a versatile platform that offers significant opportunities for both B2B and B2C marketing. Its professional focus, advanced targeting options, and affluent user base make it an essential tool for reaching and engaging with your ideal audience. By understanding the unique advantages LinkedIn offers for each type of marketing and implementing tailored strategies, you can maximize your success on this powerful professional networking platform.

1.3 Setting Up a Professional LinkedIn Profile

Creating a compelling and professional LinkedIn profile is the first step in leveraging the platform's full potential for marketing and networking. Your profile serves as your digital business card, and it needs to reflect your personal brand, skills, and professional achievements. A well-crafted profile can attract potential clients, partners, employers, and other valuable connections. Here's how to set up a professional LinkedIn profile that stands out.

Step-by-Step Guide to Setting Up Your LinkedIn Profile

1. **Profile Picture and Background Image**

- **Profile Picture**: Use a high-quality, professional headshot. Ensure you are dressed appropriately for your industry and that the photo is clear and well-lit. Profiles with photos receive significantly more views and connection requests.
- **Background Image**: Choose a background image that reflects your professional field or personal brand. This could be a branded graphic, an image of you in a professional setting, or something relevant to your industry.

2. Headline

Your headline is one of the first things people see on your profile. It should be more than just your job title; it should convey your professional identity and what you offer. For example:

- Instead of "Marketing Manager," use "Marketing Manager | Helping Businesses Grow through Data-Driven Strategies."

3. Summary (About Section)

The summary section allows you to introduce yourself in a personal and engaging way. It should be a concise narrative that highlights your career achievements, skills, and professional goals. Consider the following structure:

- **Introduction**: Start with a strong opening that captures your professional ethos.
- **Career Overview**: Provide a brief overview of your career path, key roles, and major accomplishments.
- **Skills and Expertise**: Highlight your core skills and areas of expertise.
- **Call to Action**: Conclude with a call to action, such as encouraging profile visitors to connect with you or visit your website.

Example:

"I am a seasoned marketing professional with over 10 years of experience in developing and executing data-driven strategies that drive business growth. My expertise lies in digital marketing, content creation, and lead generation. I am passionate about helping businesses enhance their online presence and achieve their marketing goals. Let's connect to explore how we can collaborate."

4. Experience

List your current and previous roles, focusing on your achievements and responsibilities rather than just job duties. Use bullet points for readability and include quantifiable results when possible:

Job Title, Company Name

- Time Period
- Achievements and Responsibilities
- Key Projects and Results (e.g., "Increased website traffic by 40% through targeted content marketing strategies.")

5. Skills and Endorsements

Add relevant skills to your profile. These should reflect your expertise and the skills that are most valued in your industry. Encourage your connections to endorse you for these skills to build credibility. LinkedIn allows you to pin your top three skills, so choose the ones most relevant to your career goals.

6. Recommendations

Request recommendations from colleagues, supervisors, and clients who can vouch for your skills and professional qualities. Recommendations add a layer of credibility and provide third-party validation of your abilities.

7. Education and Certifications

List your educational background, including degrees earned, institutions attended, and any relevant coursework or honors. Additionally, include any professional certifications that enhance your profile.

8. Volunteer Experience and Causes

Including volunteer work and causes you care about can humanize your profile and show that you are engaged in your community. This can also highlight transferable skills and demonstrate a well-rounded character.

9. Accomplishments

This section can include various achievements, such as publications, patents, projects, awards, test scores, languages, and more. Highlighting these accomplishments can differentiate you from others in your field.

10. Interests

Follow companies, influencers, and groups related to your industry. This not only shows that you are actively engaged in your professional community but also helps you stay updated on industry trends and developments.

Optimizing Your LinkedIn Profile

Once your profile is set up, there are several ways to optimize it for better visibility and engagement:

- **SEO Optimization**: Use relevant keywords throughout your profile to improve your search ranking. Think about the terms potential clients or employers might use to find someone with your skills and expertise.
- **Regular Updates**: Keep your profile up to date with new roles, projects, skills, and achievements. Regular updates signal to your network that you are active and progressing in your career.
- **Engagement**: Actively engage with your network by sharing content, commenting on posts, and participating in discussions. This increases your visibility and helps build relationships.

- **Multimedia**: Enhance your profile by adding multimedia elements such as videos, presentations, and links to your work. This makes your profile more dynamic and engaging.

Setting up a professional LinkedIn profile is crucial for making a strong first impression in the professional world. By carefully crafting each section and regularly optimizing your profile, you can enhance your brand, attract valuable connections, and open up new opportunities for career growth and business development. A well-maintained LinkedIn profile not only showcases your achievements but also serves as a platform for ongoing professional engagement and networking.

1.4 Creating a Compelling Company Page

A compelling LinkedIn company page is essential for establishing your brand's presence on the platform, engaging with your audience, and attracting potential clients and employees. Your company page should effectively communicate your brand's identity, values, and offerings. Here's a step-by-step guide to creating a company page that stands out on LinkedIn.

Step-by-Step Guide to Creating Your LinkedIn Company Page

1. Set Up Your Company Page

To create a company page, you need a personal LinkedIn profile with a verified email address associated with your company. Once you have that, follow these steps:

- Click the "Work" icon in the top right corner of your LinkedIn homepage.
- Select "Create a Company Page" from the drop-down menu.
- Choose the appropriate page type (Small business, Medium to large business, Showcase page, Educational institution).
- Enter your company's details, including name, LinkedIn public URL, website, industry, company size, and type.

2. Upload High-Quality Visuals

- **Logo**: Use a high-quality image of your company's logo. This will be your page's profile picture and will appear in searches and posts.
- **Cover Image**: Choose a visually appealing and relevant cover image that reflects your brand's identity. This could be a branded graphic, a photo of your team, or an image of your products.

3. Write a Captivating About Section

The About section is where you introduce your company to your audience. It should be concise, engaging, and informative. Include the following elements:

- **Company Description**: Briefly describe what your company does, its mission, and its values.
- **Specialties**: List your key products, services, or areas of expertise.
- **Website URL**: Provide a link to your company's website.
- **Phone Number**: Include a contact number for business inquiries.

- **Location**: Add your company's headquarters or primary location.

Example:

"XYZ Corporation is a leading provider of innovative tech solutions, dedicated to helping businesses streamline their operations and achieve their goals. Our mission is to deliver cutting-edge technology with exceptional customer service. Specialties include cloud computing, cybersecurity, and data analytics. Visit us at www.xyzcorp.com or contact us at (555) 123-4567. Located in Silicon Valley, CA."

4. Add a Strong Call to Action (CTA)

Include a clear and compelling CTA on your company page to encourage visitors to take action. This could be to visit your website, contact your sales team, or follow your page for updates. LinkedIn allows you to customize the CTA button text to align with your goals.

5. Showcase Your Products and Services

Create showcase pages for your key products or services. Showcase pages are extensions of your company page designed to highlight specific aspects of your business. They allow you to target different audience segments with tailored content.

6. Post Engaging Content Regularly

Maintaining an active presence on your company page is crucial for keeping your audience engaged. Share a variety of content types to keep your page dynamic and interesting:

- **Company News**: Announce new products, services, or company milestones.
- **Industry Insights**: Share articles, research, and insights related to your industry.
- **Employee Spotlights**: Highlight your employees and their achievements to humanize your brand.
- **Customer Success Stories**: Share testimonials and case studies that showcase how your products or services have benefited your customers.
- **Multimedia Content**: Use images, videos, and infographics to make your posts more engaging.

7. Utilize LinkedIn Analytics

LinkedIn provides analytics tools to help you understand how your company page is performing. Use these insights to refine your strategy and improve engagement:

- **Visitor Analytics**: Track the number of visitors, their demographics, and how they found your page.
- **Follower Analytics**: Analyze the growth of your followers and their engagement with your content.

- **Content Analytics**: Measure the performance of your posts, including likes, shares, comments, and click-through rates.

Best Practices for a Successful Company Page

1. Optimize for Search

Ensure your company page is optimized for search engines by incorporating relevant keywords in your company description, specialties, and updates. This will improve your page's visibility both on LinkedIn and in external search engine results.

2. Engage with Your Audience

Respond to comments on your posts and engage with followers who share or comment on your content. This interaction helps build a community around your brand and fosters stronger relationships with your audience.

3. Leverage Employee Advocacy

Encourage your employees to engage with and share your company's content. Employee advocacy can significantly expand your reach and lend authenticity to your brand's messaging.

4. Showcase Company Culture

Share content that reflects your company culture, values, and work environment. This can attract potential employees who align with your company's ethos and are excited about joining your team.

5. Consistency is Key

Maintain a consistent posting schedule to keep your audience engaged. Regular updates show that your company is active and committed to providing value to its followers.

Creating a compelling LinkedIn company page is essential for establishing a strong online presence and engaging with your target audience. By following these steps and best practices, you can create a page that effectively communicates your brand's identity, attracts potential clients and employees, and drives business growth. A well-maintained company page is a powerful tool for building credibility, showcasing your expertise, and fostering meaningful connections in the professional world.

1.5 Defining Your LinkedIn Marketing Goals

Before diving into LinkedIn marketing strategies, it's crucial to define your marketing goals. Clear, specific goals provide direction, help measure success, and guide your LinkedIn activities. Whether your aim is brand awareness, lead generation, or thought leadership, setting well-defined objectives will ensure your efforts are focused and effective.

Why Defining Goals is Important

Defining your LinkedIn marketing goals is essential for several reasons:

- **Focus**: Clear goals help you concentrate your efforts on the most impactful activities.
- **Measurement**: Specific goals enable you to track progress and measure success.
- **Alignment**: Goals align your LinkedIn activities with broader business objectives.
- **Resource Allocation**: Defined goals help allocate resources efficiently, ensuring that time and budget are spent on high-impact initiatives.

Common LinkedIn Marketing Goals

LinkedIn can support a variety of marketing goals, each requiring different strategies and tactics. Here are some common goals and the strategies to achieve them:

1. Brand Awareness

Objective: Increase the visibility and recognition of your brand among LinkedIn users.

Strategies:

- **Content Sharing**: Regularly post high-quality content that highlights your brand's values, products, and services.
- **Engagement**: Participate in discussions, comment on relevant posts, and engage with your audience to increase your brand's visibility.
- **Sponsored Content**: Use LinkedIn Ads to promote your content to a broader audience.
- **Employee Advocacy**: Encourage employees to share company updates and content to expand reach.

Metrics to Track:

- Post impressions
- Profile and page views
- Follower growth
- Engagement rates (likes, shares, comments)

2. Lead Generation

Objective: Attract and capture leads for your sales pipeline.

Strategies:

- **Lead Magnets**: Offer valuable resources such as whitepapers, ebooks, and webinars in exchange for contact information.
- **LinkedIn Ads**: Utilize Sponsored Content, Sponsored InMail, and Lead Gen Forms to target potential leads.
- **Connection Building**: Actively connect with potential leads and engage with their content to build relationships.
- **Personalized Messaging**: Use personalized InMail messages to reach out to potential leads directly.

Metrics to Track:

- Number of leads generated
- Click-through rates (CTR) on ads and content
- Conversion rates
- Cost per lead (CPL)

3. Thought Leadership

Objective: Establish yourself or your company as an authority in your industry.

Strategies:

- **Content Creation**: Publish insightful articles, research findings, and thought-provoking posts.
- **Speaking Engagements**: Share experiences from industry events, webinars, and conferences.

- **LinkedIn Live**: Host live sessions to discuss industry trends and share expertise.
- **Engagement in Groups**: Participate in relevant LinkedIn Groups and contribute valuable insights.

Metrics to Track:

- Content engagement (likes, shares, comments)
- Number of article views
- Follower growth
- Invitations to speak at events or write guest posts

4. Recruitment

Objective: Attract and hire top talent for your organization.

Strategies:

- **Job Postings**: Use LinkedIn's job posting features to advertise open positions.
- **Employer Branding**: Share content that showcases your company culture, employee experiences, and workplace achievements.
- **Employee Advocacy**: Encourage employees to share job openings and refer candidates.
- **Networking**: Connect with potential candidates and engage with their content.

Metrics to Track:

- Number of applicants
- Quality of applicants
- Time to fill positions
- Engagement with recruitment posts

5. Customer Engagement and Retention

Objective: Build stronger relationships with existing customers and keep them engaged.

Strategies:

- **Customer Stories**: Share testimonials, case studies, and success stories.
- **Interactive Content**: Post polls, ask questions, and create content that encourages engagement.
- **Regular Updates**: Keep your audience informed about new products, features, and company news.
- **Customer Support**: Use LinkedIn as a channel for addressing customer inquiries and feedback.

Metrics to Track:

- Engagement rates

- Customer feedback and comments
- Number of repeat interactions
- Customer satisfaction scores

Setting SMART Goals

To ensure your LinkedIn marketing goals are effective, use the SMART criteria:

- **Specific**: Clearly define what you want to achieve.
- **Measurable**: Establish criteria to measure progress and success.
- **Achievable**: Set realistic goals that are attainable with available resources.
- **Relevant**: Ensure goals align with broader business objectives.
- **Time-bound**: Set deadlines for achieving your goals.

Example of SMART Goals

- **Brand Awareness**: Increase the company's LinkedIn page followers by 20% within the next six months.
- **Lead Generation**: Generate 50 new leads per month through LinkedIn Ads and content marketing.
- **Thought Leadership**: Publish two industry-related articles per month and achieve at least 500 views on each.
- **Recruitment**: Fill three key positions within the next quarter using LinkedIn's job posting and networking features.

- **Customer Engagement**: Achieve an engagement rate of 10% on all customer-related posts within the next quarter.

Defining clear LinkedIn marketing goals is a crucial step in creating a successful marketing strategy. By understanding what you want to achieve and setting specific, measurable, achievable, relevant, and time-bound goals, you can focus your efforts, track your progress, and align your activities with your broader business objectives. With well-defined goals, your LinkedIn marketing efforts will be more targeted, effective, and ultimately more successful.

Chapter 2: Building and Optimizing Your LinkedIn Network

Building and optimizing your LinkedIn network is essential for maximizing your presence on the platform and achieving your marketing goals. Your network consists of connections, followers, and engagement that collectively contribute to your influence and reach within your industry. This chapter explores strategies for effectively expanding your network and optimizing your connections for meaningful engagement and business growth.

Understanding LinkedIn Connections

LinkedIn connections are the foundation of your network. They include colleagues, clients, industry peers, and potential leads or partners. Building a robust network involves strategically connecting with individuals who can contribute to your professional development and business objectives.

Strategies for Building Your LinkedIn Network

1. Optimize Your Profile:

A complete and professional profile attracts more connections. Ensure your profile picture, headline, summary, and experience sections are compelling and up-to-date.

2. Search and Connect:

Use LinkedIn's search features to find professionals in your industry, target market, or geographic area. Send personalized connection requests that highlight mutual interests or shared connections.

3. Engage with Content:

Like, comment on, and share relevant content to increase your visibility and attract potential connections. Engage thoughtfully to spark conversations and build relationships.

4. Join LinkedIn Groups:

Participate in industry-specific groups to connect with like-minded professionals, share insights, and expand your network organically.

5. Attend and Host Events:

Attend virtual or in-person events hosted by LinkedIn or industry organizations. Hosting your events, such as webinars or networking sessions, can also attract connections.

Optimizing Your LinkedIn Connections

1. Personalize Connection Requests:

When sending connection requests, personalize your message to explain why you want to connect and how you can provide value to the recipient.

2. Maintain Regular Engagement:

Stay active on LinkedIn by sharing updates, articles, and industry news. Engage with your connections' posts through comments and shares to foster stronger relationships.

3. Offer Value:

Share knowledge, insights, and resources that are valuable to your network. Position yourself as a helpful resource and industry expert.

4. Utilize LinkedIn's Features:

Take advantage of LinkedIn's features like InMail, endorsements, and recommendations to enhance your credibility and strengthen connections.

5. Segment Your Network:

Organize your connections into lists or categories based on factors like industry, location, or relationship status. This segmentation can help you tailor your interactions and content more effectively.

Leveraging LinkedIn for Business Growth

1. Lead Generation:

Use your expanded network to generate leads through content marketing, targeted messaging, and LinkedIn Ads.

2. Partnerships and Collaborations:

Identify potential partners or collaborators within your network who can help you expand your business reach or offer complementary services.

3. Recruitment:

Tap into your network to recruit top talent for your organization. Share job postings and leverage employee referrals.

4. Brand Advocacy:

Encourage your network to advocate for your brand by sharing your content and recommending your products or services.

Building and optimizing your LinkedIn network is a continuous process that requires active engagement, strategic connections, and providing value to your connections. By expanding your network thoughtfully and nurturing relationships through meaningful interactions, you can enhance your professional reputation, increase your influence in your industry, and unlock new opportunities for business growth and success. In the following chapters, we will delve deeper into specific tactics and strategies to leverage your LinkedIn network effectively for various marketing objectives.

2.1 Identifying Your Target Audience

Identifying your target audience on LinkedIn is crucial for creating effective marketing campaigns and building meaningful connections. Your target audience consists of individuals or businesses who are most likely to be interested in your products, services, or content. By understanding and defining your target audience, you can tailor your LinkedIn strategy to reach and engage with the right people effectively.

Steps to Identify Your Target Audience

1. Define Demographics:

Start by identifying the demographic characteristics of your ideal audience. Consider factors such as age, gender, location, job title, industry, company size, and seniority level. This information helps you narrow down who your potential audience is on LinkedIn.

2. Understand Psychographics:

Psychographic factors include interests, values, attitudes, lifestyle, and behaviors. Understanding these aspects helps you create content and messaging that resonates with your audience's motivations and preferences.

3. Research LinkedIn Insights:

Use LinkedIn's analytics and audience insights tools to gather data about your current followers and engagement metrics. This information can provide valuable insights into who is already engaging with your content and help refine your target audience.

4. Survey Your Existing Customers:

If applicable, survey your existing customers to understand their demographics, preferences, and why they chose your products or services. This data can help you identify similar prospects on LinkedIn.

5. Competitor Analysis:

Analyze your competitors' LinkedIn presence to identify their target audience and engagement strategies. Look at who is following them, engaging with their content, and interacting with their brand.

Creating Buyer Personas

Once you have gathered sufficient information, create detailed buyer personas that represent different segments of your target audience. A buyer persona typically includes:

- **Name and Job Title**: Give your persona a name and specify their job title or role.
- **Demographic Details**: Include age, gender, location, and other relevant demographic information.
- **Goals and Challenges**: Describe their professional goals, the challenges they face, and what they are looking to achieve.
- **Psychographic Insights**: Detail their interests, values, motivations, and behaviors related to their industry or profession.
- **Preferred Content and Channels**: Identify the type of content they engage with and the LinkedIn groups or pages they follow.
- **Buying Behavior**: Understand their decision-making process and factors that influence their purchasing decisions.

Tailoring Your LinkedIn Strategy

Armed with insights from your target audience analysis and buyer personas, tailor your LinkedIn strategy to effectively reach and engage with your ideal audience. Consider the following tactics:

- **Content Creation**: Develop content that addresses your audience's pain points, interests, and goals. Use language and messaging that resonates with them.
- **Targeted Advertising**: Utilize LinkedIn Ads to target specific demographics and interests based on your audience analysis.
- **Networking and Engagement**: Connect with individuals who fit your buyer personas and engage with their content to build relationships.
- **Thought Leadership**: Share industry insights and thought leadership content that positions your brand as a valuable resource to your target audience.

Identifying your target audience on LinkedIn is fundamental to the success of your marketing efforts on the platform. By understanding who your ideal customers or clients are, you can create more relevant and targeted content, engage effectively with your audience, and ultimately achieve your business objectives. Continuously monitor and refine your audience targeting strategies based on feedback and analytics to optimize your LinkedIn marketing performance.

2.2 Growing Your Professional Network

Growing your professional network on LinkedIn is essential for expanding your reach, fostering valuable connections, and unlocking new opportunities. Whether you're aiming to build industry influence, generate leads, or explore career prospects, strategically growing your network can significantly enhance your LinkedIn experience and overall professional growth.

Strategies for Growing Your LinkedIn Network

1. Optimize Your Profile for Connection Requests:

Ensure your LinkedIn profile is complete, professional, and showcases your expertise. A compelling profile increases the likelihood of receiving connection requests.

2. Connect with Colleagues and Alumni:

Start by connecting with current and former colleagues, classmates, and alumni from your university. These connections often form the foundation of your professional network.

3. Utilize LinkedIn's Search Functionality:

Use LinkedIn's search filters to find professionals who align with your industry, interests, or career goals. Send personalized connection requests highlighting mutual interests or shared connections.

4. Join and Engage in LinkedIn Groups:

Participate actively in LinkedIn Groups relevant to your industry or professional interests. Engage in discussions, share insights, and connect with group members who share common interests.

5. Attend and Participate in Events:

Attend virtual or in-person events such as webinars, industry conferences, and networking sessions hosted on LinkedIn. Engage with participants and speakers to expand your network.

6. Follow Influencers and Thought Leaders:

Follow industry influencers and thought leaders on LinkedIn. Engage with their content by liking, commenting, and sharing to increase your visibility within their networks.

7. Engage with Your Network's Connections:

Explore mutual connections through your existing network. Request introductions to individuals who align with your professional goals and interests.

Best Practices for Growing Your Network

1. Personalize Connection Requests:

When sending connection requests, personalize your message to explain why you're interested in connecting and how you can provide value to the recipient.

2. Be Genuine and Authentic:

Build genuine relationships by showing interest in others' work, sharing relevant content, and offering help or insights when appropriate.

3. Stay Active and Consistent:

Maintain an active presence on LinkedIn by sharing updates, articles, and industry news. Consistent engagement keeps you visible and top-of-mind among your connections.

4. Offer Value to Your Network:

Share valuable insights, resources, and industry knowledge that benefit your connections. Position yourself as a helpful resource within your professional community.

5. Leverage Recommendations and Endorsements:

Request and provide endorsements for skills and recommendations for colleagues and connections. This helps build credibility and trust within your network.

Networking Etiquette on LinkedIn

1. Respect Personal Boundaries:

Be mindful of others' preferences when sending connection requests or engaging in conversations. Respect privacy settings and professional boundaries.

2. Follow Up and Maintain Relationships:

Nurture your connections by following up after initial interactions, congratulating them on achievements, and staying connected through regular engagement.

3. Give Before You Ask:

Offer support, insights, or introductions to your network connections before seeking favors or assistance. Reciprocity strengthens relationships.

Growing your professional network on LinkedIn requires a strategic approach, active engagement, and a commitment to building meaningful relationships. By leveraging LinkedIn's features, engaging thoughtfully with your connections, and consistently adding value to your network, you can expand your influence, discover new opportunities, and enhance your career or business prospects. Continuously nurture your network by staying informed, participating in discussions, and adapting your networking strategy to align with your professional goals and aspirations.

2.3 Leveraging LinkedIn Groups

LinkedIn Groups are a powerful tool for networking, sharing knowledge, and establishing your professional presence in your industry. By joining and actively participating in LinkedIn Groups, you can connect with like-minded professionals, gain insights, and expand your reach. This section explores strategies for effectively leveraging LinkedIn Groups to enhance your professional network and achieve your marketing goals.

Understanding LinkedIn Groups

LinkedIn Groups are communities of professionals who share common interests, industries, or goals. They provide a platform for members to discuss relevant topics, share content, and engage in meaningful conversations. Groups can be focused on specific industries, job roles, skills, or professional interests.

Finding the Right Groups

Identifying and joining the right LinkedIn Groups is the first step toward leveraging them effectively. Here's how to find groups that align with your interests and goals:

1. Use LinkedIn's Search Feature:

Use the search bar at the top of your LinkedIn homepage to find groups related to your industry, profession, or interests. Use keywords relevant to your field to narrow down the search results.

2. Explore Group Recommendations:

LinkedIn often recommends groups based on your profile, connections, and activity. Check these recommendations regularly to discover new groups that may be of interest.

3. Check Competitors and Influencers:

Look at the profiles of competitors and industry influencers to see which groups they are members of. Joining these groups can provide valuable networking opportunities and insights.

4. Consider Niche and General Groups:

Join both niche groups focused on specific topics and broader groups related to your industry. Niche groups can offer in-depth discussions, while broader groups can provide diverse perspectives.

Participating Actively in Groups

Once you've joined relevant groups, active participation is key to leveraging their benefits. Here's how to engage effectively:

1. Introduce Yourself:

When you join a new group, introduce yourself to the members. Share a brief overview of your background, interests, and what you hope to gain from the group.

2. Share Valuable Content:

Regularly share articles, blog posts, videos, and other content that is relevant and valuable to group members. Ensure your content adds value and encourages discussion.

3. Engage in Discussions:

Participate in ongoing discussions by commenting on posts, asking questions, and sharing your insights. Engaging thoughtfully with other members' content can help establish your presence in the group.

4. Start New Conversations:

Initiate new discussions by posting questions, sharing industry news, or discussing trends. Starting conversations can position you as a thought leader and encourage others to engage with you.

5. Provide Support and Solutions:

Offer help, advice, and solutions to group members who seek assistance. Being a resourceful and supportive member can build your reputation and foster strong relationships.

Leveraging Groups for Marketing and Networking

LinkedIn Groups can also be a strategic tool for marketing and networking. Here's how to use groups to achieve your professional goals:

1. Build Brand Awareness:

Share content from your company or personal brand that demonstrates your expertise and value. Use group discussions to highlight your knowledge and insights.

2. Generate Leads:

Identify potential leads within groups by engaging with members who fit your target audience profile. Build relationships through meaningful interactions before approaching them with business propositions.

3. Conduct Market Research:

Use group discussions to gather insights into industry trends, challenges, and needs. This information can inform your marketing strategies and content creation.

4. Promote Events and Webinars:

Share information about upcoming events, webinars, or workshops hosted by your company. Engage group members by inviting them to participate and discussing event topics.

5. Network with Industry Leaders:

Connect with influencers and thought leaders in your industry by participating in the same groups. Engage with their content and contribute to discussions they initiate.

Best Practices for LinkedIn Group Participation

To maximize the benefits of LinkedIn Groups, adhere to the following best practices:

1. Follow Group Rules and Guidelines:

Each group may have its own set of rules and guidelines. Respect these rules to maintain a positive and productive environment.

2. Be Consistent:

Regular participation is key to building a presence in any group. Aim to engage with group content several times a week.

3. Stay Relevant:

Ensure your contributions are relevant to the group's focus. Avoid off-topic posts and ensure your content adds value to the group discussions.

4. Be Professional and Respectful:

Maintain a professional tone in your interactions and respect differing opinions. Constructive and respectful dialogue fosters a positive group experience.

5. Monitor Group Activity:

Regularly monitor group activity to stay informed about new discussions and trends. Use notifications to keep track of posts and comments in groups you're active in.

Leveraging LinkedIn Groups effectively can significantly enhance your professional network, expand your reach, and support your marketing goals. By joining the right groups, participating actively, and adhering to best practices, you can build valuable relationships, gain industry insights, and establish your expertise. In the following sections, we will explore advanced LinkedIn strategies to further optimize your professional networking and marketing efforts on the platform.

2.4 Building Strong Connections and Relationships

Building strong connections and relationships on LinkedIn is fundamental to leveraging the platform's full potential. Meaningful professional relationships can lead to new opportunities, partnerships, and career advancements. This section outlines strategies for cultivating and nurturing strong connections on LinkedIn, ensuring your network is engaged, valuable, and mutually beneficial.

The Importance of Strong Connections

Strong connections on LinkedIn go beyond the number of contacts in your network. They are characterized by mutual respect, trust, and ongoing interaction. Such relationships can lead to:

- Enhanced credibility and influence within your industry
- Increased visibility and engagement with your content
- Access to new business opportunities and partnerships
- A supportive network for career growth and development

Strategies for Building Strong Connections

1. Personalize Your Connection Requests:

When sending connection requests, personalize your message. Mention how you found the person, any mutual connections, and why you want to connect. A thoughtful, personalized message shows genuine interest and increases the likelihood of acceptance.

2. Engage Regularly with Your Network:

Regular engagement is key to maintaining strong relationships. Like, comment on, and share your connections' posts. Congratulate them on their achievements and milestones. Regular interaction keeps you top-of-mind and strengthens your relationships.

3. Provide Value Consistently:

Share valuable content, such as industry insights, helpful resources, and your own professional experiences. Offering value without expecting immediate returns builds goodwill and positions you as a resourceful and generous connection.

4. Be Responsive and Approachable:

Respond promptly to messages, comments, and connection requests. Being approachable and responsive fosters a positive impression and encourages ongoing interaction.

5. Leverage LinkedIn's Features:

Utilize features like endorsements and recommendations to recognize and support your connections. Endorse skills and write recommendations that highlight their strengths and contributions. This not only strengthens your relationships but also enhances your credibility.

Nurturing Relationships over Time

Building strong connections is an ongoing process that requires regular effort. Here are ways to nurture relationships over time:

1. Stay in Touch:

Periodically check in with your connections through messages or comments on their posts. A simple "hello" or "how are you?" can go a long way in maintaining relationships.

2. Offer Help and Support:

Be proactive in offering assistance, whether it's sharing job opportunities, providing introductions, or offering advice. Being supportive and helpful strengthens your network and encourages reciprocity.

3. Celebrate Successes:

Celebrate your connections' successes and milestones. Congratulate them on promotions, new jobs, and achievements. Recognition and celebration foster goodwill and deepen relationships.

4. Collaborate on Projects:

Look for opportunities to collaborate with your connections on projects, events, or content. Collaboration can strengthen bonds and lead to mutually beneficial outcomes.

5. Attend and Host Events:

Participate in or host events such as webinars, workshops, and meetups. Events provide opportunities for deeper engagement and personal interaction with your network.

Best Practices for Building and Maintaining Strong Relationships

1. Be Authentic:

Authenticity is crucial in building trust and credibility. Be genuine in your interactions, share your true thoughts and experiences, and avoid overly promotional behavior.

2. Respect Boundaries:

Respect your connections' boundaries and preferences. Avoid spamming them with messages or requests, and be mindful of their time and availability.

3. Listen Actively:

Show genuine interest in your connections by listening to their needs, challenges, and aspirations. Active listening demonstrates respect and builds deeper connections.

4. Stay Professional:

Maintain a professional tone in your interactions. While it's important to build rapport, always keep your communication respectful and professional.

5. Monitor and Reflect:

Regularly reflect on the strength of your connections and identify areas for improvement. Use LinkedIn's analytics to monitor engagement and adjust your strategy as needed.

Building strong connections and relationships on LinkedIn requires a strategic, consistent, and genuine approach. By personalizing your interactions, providing ongoing value, and nurturing relationships over time, you can create a robust and supportive professional network. Strong connections enhance your credibility, open doors to new opportunities, and contribute to your overall professional success. In the next sections, we will explore advanced techniques for maximizing the impact of your LinkedIn presence and achieving your business and career goals.

2.5 Maintaining and Nurturing Your Network

Maintaining and nurturing your LinkedIn network is crucial for fostering long-term relationships and reaping the benefits of your professional connections. While building your network lays the foundation, consistent effort in maintaining and nurturing these relationships ensures ongoing engagement and mutual support. This section provides strategies and best practices for effectively maintaining and nurturing your LinkedIn network.

The Importance of Network Maintenance

Maintaining your LinkedIn network involves staying connected with your contacts, engaging with their content, and ensuring that your interactions are meaningful. A well-maintained network can lead to:

- Enhanced professional relationships and trust
- Increased opportunities for collaboration and partnerships
- Greater visibility and engagement with your content
- A supportive community for career and business growth

Strategies for Maintaining and Nurturing Your Network

1. Regular Engagement:

Stay active on LinkedIn by regularly liking, commenting on, and sharing your connections' posts. This not only keeps you visible but also shows your support and interest in their activities.

2. Personalized Communication:

Periodically reach out to your connections through personalized messages. Congratulate them on their achievements, share relevant articles, or simply check in to maintain a personal connection.

3. Provide Value:

Continuously offer value to your network by sharing useful content, insights, and resources. Whether it's industry news, helpful tips, or your own experiences, valuable content strengthens your relationships.

4. Celebrate Milestones:

Acknowledge and celebrate your connections' milestones such as promotions, work anniversaries, and personal achievements. Congratulatory messages and comments demonstrate your genuine interest in their success.

5. Host and Attend Events:

Participate in or host LinkedIn events like webinars, live sessions, and group discussions. Events provide opportunities for deeper interaction and help you stay connected with your network more engagingly.

Best Practices for Network Maintenance

1. Be Consistent:

Consistency is key to maintaining a strong network. Regularly engage with your connections and update your LinkedIn profile to reflect your latest achievements and activities.

2. Stay Professional:

Maintain a professional tone in all your interactions. While it's important to be personable, professionalism ensures that your communications are respected and valued.

3. Show Gratitude:

Express appreciation for the support and interactions from your network. Thank your connections for endorsements, recommendations, and engagement with your content.

4. Listen and Respond:

Pay attention to what your connections are sharing and discussing. Respond thoughtfully to their posts and messages, showing that you value their perspectives and contributions.

5. Offer Help:

Be proactive in offering assistance to your connections. Whether it's providing advice, making introductions, or sharing opportunities, being helpful strengthens your relationships.

Tools and Features for Network Maintenance

LinkedIn offers several tools and features that can aid in maintaining and nurturing your network:

1. Notifications:

Use LinkedIn notifications to stay informed about your connections' updates, job changes, and milestones. This helps you engage promptly and relevantly.

2. LinkedIn Messaging:

Utilize LinkedIn's messaging feature to keep in touch with your connections. Personalized messages foster deeper connections and ongoing communication.

3. Content Sharing:

Regularly share content that is relevant and valuable to your network. Use LinkedIn's publishing platform to write articles and share insights.

4. Endorsements and Recommendations:

Endorse skills and write recommendations for your connections. This not only supports them but also strengthens your profile and credibility.

5. Analytics:

Monitor your LinkedIn analytics to understand the engagement and reach of your content. Use this data to refine your approach and ensure your interactions are impactful.

Maintaining and nurturing your LinkedIn network is a continuous process that requires consistent effort, genuine engagement, and a focus on providing value. By actively participating in your connections' professional lives, offering support, and leveraging LinkedIn's features, you can cultivate strong, lasting relationships that benefit both your career and your connections. In the upcoming sections, we will explore advanced LinkedIn strategies and techniques to further enhance your professional networking and marketing efforts on the platform.

Chapter 3: Content Marketing on LinkedIn

Content marketing on LinkedIn is a powerful strategy for establishing your brand, engaging your audience, and driving business results. With LinkedIn's vast professional network and robust publishing tools, you can effectively share your expertise, insights, and thought leadership content. This chapter delves into the principles, strategies, and best practices for successful content marketing on LinkedIn.

1. Understanding LinkedIn Content Marketing

Content marketing involves creating and sharing valuable, relevant, and consistent content to attract and engage a clearly defined audience. On LinkedIn, content marketing helps you build your professional brand, showcase your expertise, and foster relationships with your target audience. Understanding the types of content that resonate on LinkedIn and how to leverage them is essential for success.

2. Types of Content on LinkedIn

LinkedIn supports various content formats, each with unique benefits. Here's an overview of the primary content types and how to use them effectively:

Articles:

LinkedIn's publishing platform allows you to write long-form articles. These are ideal for sharing in-depth insights, thought leadership, and comprehensive analyses. Articles can position you as an expert in your field and drive engagement through comments and shares.

Posts:

Regular posts on your feed can include text updates, images, videos, and links. These shorter pieces of content are perfect for sharing quick insights, industry news, personal experiences, and engaging visuals.

Videos:

Video content tends to generate high engagement on LinkedIn. Use videos to share tutorials, interviews, company updates, and behind-the-scenes looks. Ensure your videos are professional, and concise, and provide value to your audience.

Slideshows and Documents:

Upload presentations, slideshows, and documents directly to LinkedIn. These formats are excellent for sharing detailed information, infographics, case studies, and reports. They are particularly effective for B2B marketing.

Live Streams:

LinkedIn Live allows you to broadcast live video content. Use live streams for webinars, Q&A sessions, product launches, and live events. Live content fosters real-time interaction and engagement with your audience.

3. Developing a Content Strategy

A well-defined content strategy is crucial for maximizing your impact on LinkedIn. Follow these steps to create an effective content marketing strategy:

Define Your Goals:

Identify what you aim to achieve with your content marketing efforts. Common goals include increasing brand awareness, generating leads, driving website traffic, and establishing thought leadership.

Identify Your Audience:

Understand your target audience's demographics, interests, and pain points. Create buyer personas to guide your content creation and ensure your content resonates with your audience.

Plan Your Content Calendar:

Develop a content calendar to schedule your posts and articles. Consistency is key, so plan a mix of content types and topics to keep your audience engaged.

Create High-Quality Content:

Focus on producing high-quality, valuable content that addresses your audience's needs and interests. Use compelling headlines, engaging visuals, and clear, concise writing.

Optimize for LinkedIn:

Tailor your content for the LinkedIn platform. Use relevant hashtags, tag relevant connections and companies, and ensure your content is mobile-friendly.

4. Engaging Your Audience

Engagement is a critical component of content marketing on LinkedIn. Here's how to maximize audience engagement:

Encourage Interaction:

Ask questions, solicit feedback, and invite your audience to comment and share their thoughts. Engagement prompts can significantly increase interaction on your posts.

Respond to Comments:

Actively respond to comments on your posts and articles. Engaging in conversations with your audience builds relationships and demonstrates your commitment to your community.

Share User-Generated Content:

Encourage your audience to share their experiences and content related to your brand. User-generated content can enhance credibility and foster a sense of community.

Leverage Analytics:

Use LinkedIn's analytics tools to monitor the performance of your content. Track metrics such as views, likes, comments, and shares to understand what resonates with your audience and adjust your strategy accordingly.

5. Measuring Content Marketing Success

Measuring the success of your content marketing efforts on LinkedIn is essential for refining your strategy and achieving your goals. Key performance indicators (KPIs) to monitor include:

Engagement Metrics:

Track likes, comments, shares, and views to gauge how well your content is engaging your audience.

Follower Growth:

Monitor the growth of your LinkedIn followers to assess the reach and impact of your content.

Lead Generation:

Measure the number of leads generated through your LinkedIn content. Use LinkedIn's lead gen forms and track conversions from your posts and articles.

Website Traffic:

Use analytics tools to track traffic to your website from LinkedIn. Monitor metrics such as click-through rates and time spent on your site.

Brand Awareness:

Assess changes in brand awareness by tracking mentions, shares, and the reach of your content.

Content marketing on LinkedIn is a powerful way to connect with your target audience, showcase your expertise, and drive business results. By understanding the different types of content, developing a robust content strategy, engaging your audience, and measuring your success, you can effectively leverage LinkedIn for your content marketing efforts. In the following chapters, we will explore advanced LinkedIn marketing techniques and strategies to further enhance your professional presence and achieve your marketing goals on the platform.

3.1 Developing a Content Strategy

A well-developed content strategy is the backbone of successful content marketing on LinkedIn. It provides direction, consistency, and purpose to your efforts, ensuring that you're content resonates with your target audience and achieves your marketing goals. This section outlines the key steps to create an effective LinkedIn content strategy.

Define Your Goals

The first step in developing a content strategy is to clearly define your goals. Knowing what you want to achieve will guide your content creation and distribution efforts. Common goals for LinkedIn content marketing include:

- **Increasing Brand Awareness**: Expand your brand's reach and make your business more recognizable.
- **Generating Leads**: Attract potential customers and encourage them to engage with your business.
- **Driving Website Traffic**: Direct LinkedIn users to your website to increase visits and engagement.
- **Establishing Thought Leadership**: Position yourself or your company as an expert in your industry.
- **Engaging Your Audience**: Foster interaction and build a community around your brand.

Identify Your Target Audience

Understanding your target audience is crucial for creating content that resonates with them. Identify the demographics, interests, pain points, and behaviors of your ideal LinkedIn audience. Consider the following:

- **Industry and Job Roles**: Determine the industries and job titles that are most relevant to your business.
- **Demographics**: Consider factors such as age, location, and education level.
- **Interests and Challenges**: Understand what topics your audience cares about and the challenges they face.
- **Content Preferences**: Identify the types of content your audience prefers, such as articles, videos, or infographics.

Plan Your Content Calendar

A content calendar helps you organize and schedule your content consistently. Planning ensures that you maintain a regular posting schedule and cover a variety of topics. When creating your content calendar, consider the following:

- **Content Frequency**: Decide how often you will post content. Aim for consistency, whether it's daily, weekly, or bi-weekly.
- **Content Themes**: Identify key themes or topics that align with your goals and audience interests. This can include industry news, tips, case studies, and more.
- **Content Types**: Plan a mix of content types, such as articles, posts, videos, and documents, to keep your audience engaged.
- **Seasonal and Timely Content**: Incorporate seasonal themes and timely content relevant to current events or industry trends.

Create High-Quality Content

The quality of your content is paramount to its success. High-quality content is engaging, informative, and relevant to your audience. Follow these guidelines to create compelling content:

- **Provide Value**: Ensure your content addresses your audience's needs and provides actionable insights.
- **Be Authentic**: Share genuine experiences and insights. Authenticity builds trust and credibility.

- **Use Compelling Visuals**: Incorporate images, videos, infographics, and other visual elements to enhance your content.
- **Write Clearly and Concisely**: Use clear, concise language that is easy to understand. Avoid jargon unless it is commonly understood by your audience.
- **Include a Call to Action (CTA)**: Encourage your audience to take action, whether it's commenting, sharing, visiting your website, or downloading a resource.

Optimize for LinkedIn

Tailoring your content for LinkedIn's platform and audience is essential for maximizing its impact. Here are some optimization tips:

- **Use Relevant Hashtags**: Incorporate relevant hashtags to increase the discoverability of your content.
- **Tag People and Companies**: Mention relevant connections and companies in your posts to increase engagement and reach.
- **Create Engaging Headlines**: Craft attention-grabbing headlines that encourage users to click and read your content.
- **Keep Mobile in Mind**: Ensure your content is mobile-friendly, as many LinkedIn users access the platform via mobile devices.
- **Leverage LinkedIn's Features**: Use features like LinkedIn Articles for long-form content, LinkedIn Live for live videos, and Document Sharing for presentations and PDFs.

Monitor and Adjust Your Strategy

Regularly monitoring the performance of your content is crucial for refining your strategy and ensuring it remains effective. Use LinkedIn's analytics tools to track key metrics such as engagement, reach, and conversions. Consider the following:

- **Engagement Rates**: Monitor likes, comments, shares, and clicks to gauge how well your content is resonating.
- **Follower Growth**: Track the growth of your LinkedIn followers to assess the reach and impact of your content.
- **Lead Generation**: Measure the number of leads generated through your content and assess the quality of those leads.
- **Website Traffic**: Use tools like Google Analytics to track traffic from LinkedIn to your website and monitor user behavior.
- **Feedback and Insights**: Pay attention to feedback from your audience and use it to improve your content strategy.

Developing a robust content strategy for LinkedIn is essential for achieving your marketing goals and building a strong professional presence on the platform. By defining your goals, understanding your audience, planning a diverse content calendar, creating high-quality content, optimizing for LinkedIn, and regularly monitoring your performance, you can effectively leverage LinkedIn for content marketing success. In the following sections, we will explore advanced techniques and strategies to further enhance your LinkedIn content marketing efforts.

3.2 Types of Content that Work Best on LinkedIn

Creating content that resonates with your audience on LinkedIn is crucial for achieving your marketing goals. The platform supports various content formats, each offering unique ways to engage with professionals and showcase your expertise. In this section, we will explore the types of content that work best on LinkedIn and how to use them effectively.

Articles

LinkedIn's publishing platform allows you to write and share long-form articles. These are ideal for:

- **Thought Leadership**: Share in-depth insights and analyses on industry trends, challenges, and solutions. Thought leadership articles position you as an expert in your field.
- **How-To Guides**: Provide step-by-step guides and tutorials that offer practical advice and solutions to common problems faced by your audience.
- **Case Studies**: Showcase detailed examples of how your products or services have helped clients achieve their goals. Case studies build credibility and provide proof of your capabilities.
- **Opinion Pieces**: Share your perspectives on current events, industry developments, and future trends. Opinion pieces can spark discussions and engage your audience.

Short Posts

Regular posts on your feed keep your audience engaged with bite-sized content. These can include:

- **Text Updates**: Share quick insights, industry news, personal experiences, and motivational quotes. Keep text updates concise and impactful.
- **Images**: Use high-quality images to capture attention and convey your message visually. Infographics, behind-the-scenes photos, and event highlights are popular choices.
- **Polls**: Create polls to engage your audience and gather feedback on relevant topics. Polls encourage interaction and can provide valuable insights into your audience's preferences.

Videos

Video content is highly engaging and effective on LinkedIn. Use videos for:

- **Tutorials and Demos**: Showcase how to use your products or services through step-by-step demonstrations. Tutorial videos are informative and can help potential customers understand your offerings better.
- **Interviews**: Conduct interviews with industry experts, thought leaders, and satisfied customers. Interviews provide diverse perspectives and valuable insights.

- **Company Updates**: Share updates about your company, including new product launches, achievements, and behind-the-scenes looks. Company update videos humanize your brand and build a connection with your audience.

SlideShares and Documents

SlideShares and documents are perfect for sharing detailed information in an easily digestible format. These can include:

- **Presentations**: Upload slide decks from webinars, conferences, and internal meetings. Presentations can cover a wide range of topics and provide in-depth knowledge.
- **Whitepapers**: Share whitepapers that offer comprehensive analyses, research findings, and strategic insights. Whitepapers are valuable resources that can establish your authority in your industry.
- **Reports and Case Studies**: Publish detailed reports and case studies that highlight your expertise and success stories. These documents provide evidence of your capabilities and results.

LinkedIn Live

LinkedIn Live allows you to broadcast live video content, providing real-time interaction with your audience. Use LinkedIn Live for:

- **Webinars**: Host live webinars on relevant topics, featuring expert speakers and interactive Q&A sessions. Webinars can educate your audience and generate leads.
- **Q&A Sessions**: Conduct live Q&A sessions where you answer questions from your audience in real time. These sessions build engagement and trust.
- **Event Coverage**: Stream live from industry events, conferences, and company gatherings. Live event coverage provides a dynamic way to share experiences with your network.

Stories

LinkedIn Stories, similar to Instagram and Facebook Stories, offer a way to share ephemeral content. Use Stories for:

- **Daily Updates**: Share quick updates, behind-the-scenes moments, and highlights from your day. Stories keep your audience engaged with fresh, short-lived content.
- **Promotions**: Announce upcoming events, product launches, and special offers. Stories are perfect for creating urgency and excitement.
- **Employee Spotlights**: Feature your team members and their contributions. Employee spotlights humanize your brand and showcase your company culture.

Best Practices for Effective Content

Regardless of the content type, following these best practices will enhance the effectiveness of your LinkedIn content:

- **Be Relevant**: Ensure your content is relevant to your audience's interests and needs. Address current trends, challenges, and opportunities in your industry.
- **Be Engaging**: Use compelling headlines, visuals, and storytelling techniques to capture attention and encourage interaction.
- **Be Consistent**: Maintain a regular posting schedule to keep your audience engaged and establish a reliable presence.
- **Be Authentic**: Share genuine insights, experiences, and perspectives. Authenticity builds trust and credibility with your audience.
- **Be Data-Driven**: Use LinkedIn's analytics tools to monitor the performance of your content. Analyze metrics such as engagement, reach, and conversions to refine your strategy.

Understanding the types of content that work best on LinkedIn and how to use them effectively is crucial for achieving your marketing goals on the platform. By leveraging articles, short posts, videos, SlideShares, LinkedIn Live, and Stories, you can create a diverse and engaging content strategy that resonates with your audience. In the next sections, we will delve into advanced content marketing techniques and strategies to further enhance your LinkedIn presence and drive business success.

3.3 Creating Engaging and Valuable Content

Creating engaging and valuable content on LinkedIn is essential for capturing the attention of your audience, fostering meaningful interactions, and achieving your marketing goals. This section provides guidelines and best practices for crafting content that not only attracts but also retains and delights your audience.

Understanding Engagement and Value

Engagement refers to how actively your audience interacts with your content, including likes, comments, shares, and clicks. Valuable content is content that your audience finds useful, informative, and relevant. The key to successful content marketing on LinkedIn is to create content that combines both elements, ensuring it is engaging and provides real value to your audience.

Steps to Create Engaging and Valuable Content

1. **Know Your Audience**

Understanding your audience is the first step in creating content that resonates with them. Conduct research to identify their interests, pain points, and preferences. Use LinkedIn's analytics and insights tools to gather data about your audience's demographics, job roles, and engagement patterns. This information will guide your content creation process.

2. Focus on Quality

High-quality content stands out and is more likely to be shared and engaged with. Ensure your content is:

- **Well-written**: Use clear, concise, and professional language. Avoid jargon and complex sentences.
- **Accurate and Informative**: Provide factual and up-to-date information. Back your claims with data, statistics, and credible sources.
- **Visually Appealing**: Incorporate high-quality images, videos, infographics, and other visual elements to enhance your content.

3. Be Relevant

Create content that addresses the current needs and interests of your audience. Stay updated with industry trends, news, and developments to ensure your content is timely and relevant. Tailor your content to specific audience segments by addressing their unique challenges and providing targeted solutions.

4. Tell a Story

Storytelling is a powerful tool for engaging your audience. Use narratives to make your content more relatable and memorable. Share personal experiences, customer success stories, and case studies to illustrate your points and connect with your audience on an emotional level.

5. Use Strong Headlines

A compelling headline can significantly increase the chances of your content being read and shared. Craft headlines that are clear, intriguing, and promise value. Use numbers, questions, and power words to make your headlines stand out.

6. Encourage Interaction

Engage your audience by encouraging interaction and participation. Ask questions, solicit feedback, and invite your audience to share their thoughts and experiences. Use calls to action (CTAs) to prompt your audience to comment, share, or visit your website.

7. Share Insights and Expertise

Position yourself or your company as a thought leader by sharing valuable insights and expertise. Provide in-depth analyses, actionable advice, and unique perspectives on industry-related topics. Offering practical solutions and tips can establish your credibility and attract a loyal audience.

8. Leverage Visual Content

Visual content tends to generate higher engagement on LinkedIn. Use images, videos, infographics, and presentations to make your content more engaging. Ensure your visual content is of high quality and relevant to the topic you are discussing.

9. Optimize for Mobile

Many LinkedIn users access the platform via mobile devices. Ensure your content is mobile-friendly by using short paragraphs, bullet points, and large fonts. Optimize images and videos for mobile viewing to provide a seamless experience for your audience.

10. Use Hashtags and Mentions

Incorporate relevant hashtags and mentions to increase the visibility of your content. Hashtags help categorize your content and make it discoverable by users interested in specific topics. Mentioning relevant connections and companies can boost engagement and expand your content's reach.

Best Practices for Different Content Types

Articles

- **Start with a Strong Introduction**: Capture your audience's attention with a compelling opening that outlines the value of your article.
- **Use Subheadings**: Break your article into sections with clear subheadings to improve readability.
- **Include Visuals**: Enhance your article with images, charts, and infographics to support your points.
- **End with a CTA**: Encourage your readers to comment, share, or take specific actions related to the article.

Short Posts

- **Be Concise**: Keep your posts short and to the point. Aim for clarity and impact.
- **Engage with Questions**: Ask questions to prompt your audience to share their thoughts and experiences.
- **Use Emojis Sparingly**: Emojis can add personality to your posts, but use them sparingly to maintain professionalism.

Videos

- **Keep It Short**: Aim for videos that are 1-3 minutes long to maintain viewer attention.
- **Add Captions**: Include captions to make your videos accessible to a wider audience.
- **Highlight Key Points**: Use text overlays and visual cues to emphasize important information.

Creating engaging and valuable content on LinkedIn is crucial for building a strong professional presence and achieving your marketing objectives. By understanding your audience, focusing on quality and relevance, telling compelling stories, and leveraging visual content, you can craft content that captures attention and drives meaningful interactions. In the next sections, we will explore advanced content marketing techniques and strategies to further enhance your LinkedIn efforts and achieve greater success on the platform.

3.4 Leveraging LinkedIn Articles and Posts

LinkedIn offers two primary formats for sharing content: articles and posts. Each serves a different purpose and can be used strategically to enhance your content marketing efforts. This section explores how to effectively leverage LinkedIn articles and posts to maximize engagement, build your professional brand, and achieve your marketing goals.

LinkedIn Articles

LinkedIn articles are long-form content pieces that allow you to delve deeper into topics and share comprehensive insights with your audience. Here's how to make the most of LinkedIn articles:

Benefits of LinkedIn Articles

- **Thought Leadership**: Articles enable you to showcase your expertise and establish yourself as a thought leader in your industry.
- **SEO and Discoverability**: Well-written articles can appear in LinkedIn searches and Google search results, increasing your visibility.
- **In-Depth Analysis**: Articles allow for detailed exploration of topics, providing more value to your readers.
- **Long-Term Engagement**: Unlike posts, articles have a longer shelf life and can continue to attract readers and engagement over time.

Best Practices for Writing LinkedIn Articles

- **Choose Relevant Topics**: Focus on topics that are relevant to your audience and align with your expertise. Address current trends, common challenges, and emerging opportunities in your industry.
- **Craft a Compelling Title**: Your article title should be clear, intriguing, and promise value. Use keywords that your audience might search for.
- **Start with a Strong Introduction**: Capture your reader's attention with a compelling opening that outlines the article's value and sets the stage for what's to come.
- **Use Subheadings and Bullet Points**: Break your content into sections with clear subheadings to improve readability. Use bullet points to highlight key information.
- **Incorporate Visuals**: Enhance your article with high-quality images, charts, infographics, and videos to support your points and make the content more engaging.

- **Provide Actionable Insights**: Offer practical advice, solutions, and takeaways that your readers can apply.
- **Include a Call to Action (CTA)**: Encourage readers to engage with your content by asking them to comment, share, or follow you for more updates.
- **Promote Your Articles**: Share your articles across your LinkedIn network and other social media platforms to increase visibility and reach.

LinkedIn Posts

LinkedIn posts are shorter updates that appear in the feeds of your connections and followers. They are ideal for quick insights, updates, and engaging with your audience regularly. Here's how to effectively use LinkedIn posts:

Benefits of LinkedIn Posts

- **Frequent Engagement**: Regular posts keep your audience engaged and maintain your presence in their feeds.
- **Real-Time Interaction**: Posts allow for immediate interaction and feedback from your audience.
- **Versatility**: You can share various types of content, including text updates, images, videos, and links.
- **Increased Reach**: Posts can be easily shared by your connections, extending your reach to a broader audience.

Best Practices for Creating LinkedIn Posts

- **Be Concise**: Keep your posts short and to the point. Aim for clarity and impact in your messaging.
- **Use Engaging Visuals**: Incorporate high-quality images, videos, and infographics to capture attention and enhance your message.
- **Ask Questions**: Encourage engagement by asking questions and inviting your audience to share their thoughts and experiences.
- **Share Industry News**: Keep your audience informed by sharing relevant industry news, trends, and updates. Add your commentary to provide context and insights.
- **Highlight Achievements**: Share your professional achievements, milestones, and company updates to build credibility and foster a sense of community.
- **Use Hashtags and Mentions**: Increase the discoverability of your posts by using relevant hashtags and mentioning other LinkedIn users and companies.
- **Incorporate CTAs**: Prompt your audience to take action, such as visiting your website, registering for a webinar, or downloading a resource.

Combining Articles and Posts

To maximize your LinkedIn content strategy, combine the use of articles and posts to create a cohesive and comprehensive approach. Here's how:

- **Promote Articles with Posts**: Use short posts to promote your longer articles. Share key takeaways, quotes, or a summary with a link to the full article.

- **Engage in Follow-Up Discussions**: After publishing an article, create posts to initiate discussions around the topic. Encourage your audience to share their perspectives and experiences.
- **Repurpose Content**: Break down the key points from your articles into shorter posts. This allows you to extend the life of your content and reach different segments of your audience.
- **Use Analytics to Guide Strategy**: Monitor the performance of both your articles and posts using LinkedIn's analytics tools. Use the insights to refine your content strategy and focus on what resonates most with your audience.

Leveraging LinkedIn articles and posts effectively can significantly enhance your content marketing efforts on the platform. By creating in-depth, valuable articles and engaging timely posts, you can build your professional brand, foster meaningful interactions, and achieve your marketing goals. In the following sections, we will explore advanced techniques and strategies to further optimize your LinkedIn presence and drive business success.

3.5 Using LinkedIn Video for Maximum Impact

Video content has become one of the most powerful tools for engaging audiences on LinkedIn. It offers a dynamic and visually appealing way to convey messages, showcase expertise, and connect with your audience on a deeper level. This section explores how to effectively use LinkedIn video to achieve maximum impact.

Benefits of Using Video on LinkedIn

- **Higher Engagement**: Videos are more likely to capture attention and generate higher engagement rates compared to text or image posts.
- **Increased Reach**: LinkedIn's algorithm tends to prioritize video content, helping it reach a broader audience.
- **Enhanced Storytelling**: Videos allow for richer storytelling, enabling you to convey complex ideas and emotions more effectively.
- **Versatility**: Videos can be used for various purposes, such as product demos, thought leadership, company updates, and more.

Types of LinkedIn Videos

1. Native Videos

Native videos are videos that are directly uploaded to LinkedIn, rather than shared via a link from another platform. These videos autoplay in the feed, making them more likely to catch the viewer's attention.

- **Short Updates**: Share quick insights, tips, or updates that are under two minutes long. These videos are perfect for maintaining regular engagement with your audience.
- **Behind-the-Scenes**: Give your audience a peek behind the curtain by showcasing your company culture, office environment, or team activities.

- **Customer Testimonials**: Share stories from satisfied customers to build credibility and trust.

2. LinkedIn Live

LinkedIn Live allows you to broadcast live video content to your network in real-time. This feature is ideal for:

- **Webinars and Workshops**: Host educational sessions on relevant topics, featuring expert speakers and interactive Q&A segments.
- **Event Coverage**: Stream live from industry events, conferences, or company events to share experiences as they happen.
- **Product Launches**: Announce new products or services live, demonstrating their features and benefits to your audience.

Best Practices for Creating LinkedIn Videos

1. Plan Your Content

Before hitting the record button, take the time to plan your video content. Define your goals, target audience, and key messages. Outline a script or storyboard to ensure your video is structured and flows smoothly.

2. Keep It Short and Sweet

Attention spans on social media are short, so aim to keep your videos concise. Ideally, videos should be between 1-2 minutes long. For longer content, such as webinars, provide value early on to retain viewers.

3. Start with a Hook

Grab your audience's attention within the first few seconds. Use an intriguing statement, a compelling question, or an eye-catching visual to draw viewers in.

4. Focus on Quality

Ensure your video is of high quality, both in terms of production and content. Use good lighting, clear audio, and steady camera work. High-quality visuals and sound enhance the viewer's experience and reflect positively on your brand.

5. Add Captions

Many LinkedIn users watch videos without sound, especially in public or work environments. Adding captions makes your videos accessible and ensures your message is conveyed even without audio.

6. Include a Call to Action (CTA)

End your video with a clear and compelling CTA. Whether you want viewers to visit your website, download a resource, register for an event, or share your video, make sure your CTA is specific and actionable.

7. Optimize for Mobile

Since a significant portion of LinkedIn users access the platform via mobile devices, ensure your videos are mobile-friendly. Use a vertical or square format, which displays better on mobile screens, and keep text large and legible.

Promoting Your LinkedIn Videos

- **Post at Optimal Times**: Share your videos during times when your audience is most active on LinkedIn. Experiment with different posting times to determine what works best for your audience.
- **Engage with Your Audience**: Respond to comments and engage with viewers who interact with your video. Building a dialogue can enhance engagement and strengthen relationships.
- **Leverage Hashtags**: Use relevant hashtags to increase the discoverability of your videos. Research popular hashtags in your industry and include them in your video descriptions.
- **Cross-Promote**: Share your LinkedIn videos on other social media platforms, your website, and email newsletters to reach a wider audience.

- **Analyze Performance**: Use LinkedIn's analytics tools to track the performance of your videos. Monitor metrics such as views, engagement, and viewer demographics to refine your video strategy.

Using video on LinkedIn can significantly enhance your content marketing efforts and help you achieve maximum impact. By understanding the benefits of video, choosing the right types of videos, following best practices for creation and promotion, and leveraging LinkedIn's features, you can effectively engage your audience and achieve your marketing goals. In the next sections, we will delve into more advanced strategies and techniques to further optimize your LinkedIn presence and drive business success.

Chapter 4: LinkedIn Advertising Strategies

LinkedIn advertising offers powerful tools to reach a highly targeted audience of professionals and decision-makers. By leveraging LinkedIn's advertising platform, businesses can enhance their visibility, generate leads, and achieve their marketing objectives more effectively. This chapter explores various LinkedIn advertising strategies, from understanding the different ad formats to creating compelling ad content and optimizing campaigns for maximum ROI.

1. Understanding LinkedIn Ad Formats

LinkedIn provides several ad formats to cater to different marketing goals and audience preferences. Each format has unique advantages and use cases. Understanding these formats is crucial for selecting the right one for your campaign.

Sponsored Content

Sponsored Content appears directly in the LinkedIn feed of your target audience. It can be in the form of single-image ads, carousel ads (with multiple images), and video ads. Sponsored Content is ideal for increasing brand awareness, driving website traffic, and generating leads.

Sponsored InMail

Sponsored InMail allows you to send personalized messages directly to LinkedIn members' inboxes. These messages are delivered only when the recipient is active on LinkedIn, ensuring higher open rates. Sponsored InMail is effective for event invitations, personalized offers, and direct lead generation.

Text Ads

Text Ads are simple, straightforward ads that appear on the right-hand sidebar or at the top of LinkedIn pages. They include a short headline, description, and a small image or company logo. Text Ads are cost-effective and suitable for driving traffic to your website or landing page.

Dynamic Ads

Dynamic Ads are personalized ads that use LinkedIn member data to create customized content. These ads can include profile images and other personal information to make the ad more engaging. Dynamic Ads are great for building brand awareness and increasing follower engagement.

Display Ads

Display Ads are visual ads that appear on the LinkedIn Audience Network, reaching users beyond the LinkedIn platform. These ads are suitable for broader brand awareness campaigns.

2. Setting Up Your LinkedIn Ad Campaign

Creating an effective LinkedIn ad campaign involves several key steps, from defining your objectives to selecting your target audience and setting your budget.

Define Your Campaign Objectives

Before you start creating ads, clearly define your campaign objectives. Common objectives include:

- **Brand Awareness**: Increase visibility and recognition of your brand.
- **Lead Generation**: Capture contact information from potential customers.
- **Website Traffic**: Drive visitors to your website or landing page.
- **Engagement**: Increase interactions with your content, such as likes, shares, and comments.

Identify Your Target Audience

LinkedIn's targeting options allow you to reach a specific audience based on various criteria:

- **Location**: Target users in specific geographic regions.

- **Industry and Company Size**: Reach professionals in particular industries or companies of a certain size.
- **Job Title and Function**: Target individuals based on their job titles and functions.
- **Skills and Interests**: Reach users with specific skills or interests related to your product or service.
- **Education and Experience**: Target based on educational background and years of experience.

Set Your Budget and Bid Strategy

LinkedIn offers flexible budgeting options to suit different campaign sizes and goals. You can set a daily or total budget for your campaign. Additionally, you can choose from various bid strategies:

- **Cost Per Click (CPC)**: Pay only when someone clicks on your ad.
- **Cost Per Impression (CPM)**: Pay based on the number of times your ad is shown.
- **Cost Per Send (CPS)**: Pay for each InMail message delivered.

Create Compelling Ad Content

Effective ad content is crucial for capturing attention and driving action. Here are some tips for creating compelling LinkedIn ads:

- **Engaging Visuals**: Use high-quality images or videos that are relevant and eye-catching.

- **Clear Messaging**: Ensure your ad copy is concise, clear, and compelling. Highlight the benefits of your product or service.
- **Strong Call to Action (CTA)**: Encourage your audience to take action with a clear and persuasive CTA, such as "Learn More," "Sign Up," or "Download Now."
- **Personalization**: Tailor your ad content to the specific interests and needs of your target audience.

3. Optimizing Your LinkedIn Ad Campaign

Once your ad campaign is live, continuous monitoring and optimization are essential to maximize its performance. Here's how to optimize your LinkedIn ad campaign:

Monitor Key Metrics

Track key performance metrics to understand how your ads are performing. Important metrics include:

- **Click-Through Rate (CTR)**: The percentage of people who click on your ad after seeing it.
- **Conversion Rate**: The percentage of ad clicks that result in a desired action, such as form submissions or downloads.
- **Cost Per Conversion**: The average cost of acquiring a conversion.

A/B Testing

Conduct A/B tests to compare different versions of your ads. Test variables such as headlines, images, CTAs, and ad formats to determine what works best. Use the insights gained from these tests to refine your ad content and targeting.

Adjust Targeting

Regularly review and adjust your targeting parameters to ensure you are reaching the most relevant audience. Analyze the performance of different audience segments and refine your targeting criteria based on these insights.

Optimize Bids and Budget

Monitor your bid strategy and budget allocation to ensure you are getting the best return on investment (ROI). Adjust bids based on the performance of your ads and reallocate the budget to the highest-performing campaigns.

Use LinkedIn Insights and Analytics

Leverage LinkedIn's insights and analytics tools to gain a deeper understanding of your ad performance. Use this data to identify trends, optimize your strategy, and make informed decisions.

4. Advanced LinkedIn Advertising Strategies

To take your LinkedIn advertising to the next level, consider implementing advanced strategies that can enhance your campaign's effectiveness.

Retargeting

Use LinkedIn's retargeting options to reach users who have previously interacted with your brand. Retargeting helps reinforce your message and increases the likelihood of conversion.

Account-Based Marketing (ABM)

Implement ABM strategies to target specific companies or accounts that are most valuable to your business. Create customized ad campaigns that address the unique needs and pain points of these accounts.

Lookalike Audiences

Create lookalike audiences based on your existing customers or high-value leads. This strategy allows you to reach new potential customers who share similar characteristics with your best-performing audience segments.

Lead Gen Forms

Use LinkedIn's Lead Gen Forms to capture contact information directly within the platform. This reduces friction for users and increases the likelihood of lead generation.

LinkedIn advertising offers a wealth of opportunities to reach and engage a professional audience. By understanding the different ad formats, setting up well-defined campaigns, creating compelling content, and continuously optimizing your efforts, you can achieve significant results on the platform. In the following chapters, we will explore more advanced tactics and strategies to further enhance your LinkedIn marketing efforts and drive business success.

4.1 Understanding LinkedIn Ad Formats

LinkedIn offers a variety of ad formats to cater to different marketing goals and audience preferences. Each format has unique advantages and use cases, allowing marketers to choose the best option for their specific campaign objectives. Understanding these ad formats is crucial for designing effective LinkedIn advertising strategies.

Sponsored Content

Sponsored Content appears directly in the LinkedIn feed of your target audience. This format blends seamlessly with organic posts, making it less intrusive and more engaging. Sponsored Content comes in several variations:

- **Single Image Ads**: These ads feature one image and are ideal for sharing straightforward messages or promotions. They can drive traffic to your website, promote events, or showcase products.
- **Video Ads**: Video ads are highly engaging and allow you to tell a more comprehensive story. They are excellent for demonstrating products, sharing customer testimonials, or providing educational content.
- **Carousel Ads**: Carousel ads consist of images or videos that users can swipe through. This format is perfect for showcasing multiple products, features, or benefits in one ad.
- **Event Ads**: These ads promote events and encourage registrations. They can highlight details about upcoming webinars, conferences, or workshops.

Sponsored InMail

Sponsored InMail allows you to send personalized messages directly to LinkedIn members' inboxes. These messages are only delivered when the recipient is active on LinkedIn, ensuring higher open rates. Sponsored InMail is effective for:

- **Event Invitations**: Invite targeted professionals to attend webinars, conferences, or meetups.
- **Personalized Offers**: Send tailored offers or discounts to specific audience segments.
- **Lead Generation**: Engage directly with potential leads by offering valuable content or opportunities.

Text Ads

Text Ads are simple yet effective ads that appear on the right-hand sidebar or at the top of LinkedIn pages. They include a short headline, a brief description, and a small image or company logo. Text Ads are cost-effective and suitable for:

- **Driving Website Traffic**: Encourage users to visit your website or landing page.
- **Generating Leads**: Promote whitepapers, e-books, or other gated content to capture leads.
- **Building Brand Awareness**: Increase visibility with straightforward messaging.

Dynamic Ads

Dynamic Ads use LinkedIn member data to create personalized ad content. These ads can automatically customize their appearance based on the viewer's profile, making them more engaging. Types of Dynamic Ads include:

- **Follower Ads**: Encourage LinkedIn members to follow your company page by displaying their profile picture alongside your brand logo.
- **Spotlight Ads**: Highlight specific products, services, or offers and include a personalized call to action.
- **Content Ads**: Promote content downloads or sign-ups with personalized ad creatives.

Display Ads

Display Ads are visual ads that appear on the LinkedIn Audience Network, reaching users beyond the LinkedIn platform. These ads are suitable for broader brand awareness campaigns and can include rich media formats for higher engagement.

Message Ads

Message Ads, similar to Sponsored InMail, deliver direct messages to LinkedIn members' inboxes. However, Message Ads allow for shorter, more concise messages and are often used for:

- **Immediate Calls to Action**: Prompt users to take quick actions such as downloading a report or signing up for a newsletter.
- **Short Campaigns**: Ideal for limited-time offers or announcements.

Conversation Ads

Conversation Ads provide a more interactive experience by allowing recipients to choose their path through multiple response options. This format is ideal for:

- **Interactive Content**: Engage users with personalized, interactive content that adapts based on their responses.

- **Lead Nurturing**: Guide potential leads through a tailored journey, providing information and offers based on their choices.

Sponsored Job Posts

Sponsored Job Posts help companies promote job openings to a targeted audience. These posts appear in the LinkedIn feed and job search results, increasing the visibility of your job listings and attracting qualified candidates.

Document Ads

Document Ads allow you to share rich content, such as presentations, whitepapers, or case studies, directly in the LinkedIn feed. Users can preview the first few pages and then download the document, making it an effective tool for lead generation and sharing in-depth information.

Choosing the Right Ad Format

Selecting the right ad format depends on your specific marketing goals and the nature of your audience. Here are some considerations to help you choose:

- **Brand Awareness**: Use Sponsored Content (Single Image, Video, Carousel) and Dynamic Ads to increase visibility and engagement.

- **Lead Generation**: Leverage Sponsored InMail, Message Ads, and Lead Gen Forms to capture valuable leads.
- **Website Traffic**: Utilize Text Ads and Sponsored Content to drive users to your website or landing pages.
- **Event Promotion**: Promote events with Event Ads and Sponsored InMail.
- **Job Recruitment**: Use Sponsored Job Posts to attract top talent.

Understanding the various LinkedIn ad formats is essential for designing effective advertising campaigns. By choosing the right format based on your objectives and audience, you can maximize engagement, drive conversions, and achieve your marketing goals. In the following sections, we will explore how to set up and optimize your LinkedIn ad campaigns for optimal performance.

4.2 Setting Up and Managing LinkedIn Ads

Setting up and managing LinkedIn ads effectively involves a series of strategic steps. By following a structured approach, you can ensure that your campaigns are well-targeted, compelling, and optimized for the best possible results. This section provides a comprehensive guide on how to set up and manage LinkedIn ads, from initial planning to ongoing optimization.

Step 1: Define Your Campaign Objectives

The first step in setting up LinkedIn ads is to clearly define your campaign objectives. Your objectives will guide your ad format selection, targeting, and messaging. Common objectives include:

- **Brand Awareness**: Increase visibility and recognition of your brand among LinkedIn users.
- **Lead Generation**: Capture contact information from potential customers.
- **Website Traffic**: Drive visitors to your website or specific landing pages.
- **Engagement**: Boost interactions with your content, such as likes, shares, and comments.
- **Conversions**: Encourage specific actions, such as downloads, sign-ups, or purchases.

Step 2: Choose the Right Ad Format

Based on your campaign objectives, select the most suitable ad format. Refer to section 4.1 for a detailed overview of each format. Here's a quick summary:

- **Sponsored Content**: Ideal for brand awareness, lead generation, and engagement.
- **Sponsored InMail**: Effective for direct engagement and lead generation.
- **Text Ads**: Suitable for driving website traffic and building brand awareness.
- **Dynamic Ads**: Great for personalized engagement and follower growth.
- **Display Ads**: Useful for broad brand awareness campaigns.
- **Message Ads**: Best for concise, direct calls to action.
- **Conversation Ads**: Ideal for interactive content and lead nurturing.

- **Sponsored Job Posts**: Effective for recruiting and attracting top talent.

Step 3: Set Up Your LinkedIn Campaign

- **Access Campaign Manager**: Log in to LinkedIn Campaign Manager, LinkedIn's self-service ad platform.
- **Create a New Campaign**: Click on the "Create Campaign" button and choose your campaign objective.
- **Name Your Campaign**: Give your campaign a descriptive name to easily identify it later.
- **Select Your Ad Format**: Choose the appropriate ad format based on your objectives.
- **Define Your Target Audience**: Use LinkedIn's targeting options to specify your audience. You can target by location, industry, company size, job title, job function, skills, interests, and more. The more precise your targeting, the more relevant your ads will be to your audience.
- **Set Your Budget and Schedule**: Decide on your budget and bidding strategy. You can choose between a daily or total budget and select from Cost Per Click (CPC), Cost Per Impression (CPM), or Cost Per Send (CPS) bidding. Set your campaign start and end dates or opt for continuous running.

Step 4: Create Compelling Ad Content

- **Craft Engaging Headlines**: Your headline should be clear, compelling, and relevant to your target audience.

- **Write Persuasive Ad Copy**: Ensure your ad copy is concise and highlights the key benefits of your offer. Focus on addressing the needs and pain points of your audience.
- **Design Eye-Catching Visuals**: Use high-quality images or videos that capture attention and are relevant to your message. Ensure visuals are professional and aligned with your brand identity.
- **Include a Strong Call to Action (CTA)**: Encourage your audience to take the next step with a clear and compelling CTA. Examples include "Learn More," "Sign Up," "Download Now," and "Register Today."

Step 5: Launch and Monitor Your Campaign

- **Review and Launch**: Double-check all your campaign settings, targeting criteria, and ad content. Once you're satisfied, click the "Launch" button to start your campaign.
- **Monitor Performance**: Regularly check your campaign's performance using LinkedIn's analytics tools. Key metrics to monitor include impressions, clicks, click-through rate (CTR), conversions, and cost per conversion.

Step 6: Optimize Your Campaign

- **Analyze Data**: Use the data from your campaign performance to identify trends and insights. Determine which ads are performing well and which need improvement.
- **Adjust Targeting**: Refine your targeting criteria based on the performance data. You may need to narrow or broaden your audience to improve relevance and engagement.

- **A/B Testing**: Conduct A/B tests by creating variations of your ads. Test different headlines, images, CTAs, and targeting options to see what resonates best with your audience.
- **Optimize Bids and Budget**: Adjust your bids and budget allocation to ensure you're getting the best return on investment (ROI). Increase spending on high-performing ads and reduce or pause low-performing ones.
- **Update Ad Content**: Refresh your ad content periodically to avoid ad fatigue. Keep your messaging relevant and timely to maintain audience interest.

Step 7: Report and Learn

- **Generate Reports**: Use LinkedIn Campaign Manager to generate detailed reports on your campaign performance. Analyze key metrics and compare them against your objectives.
- **Gather Insights**: Identify what worked well and what didn't. Use these insights to inform future campaigns and continuously improve your LinkedIn advertising strategy.
- **Share Results**: If you're working with a team, share the results and insights from your campaigns. Collaborative analysis can lead to more creative and effective strategies.

By defining clear objectives, selecting the right ad formats, targeting the appropriate audience, creating compelling ad content, and regularly monitoring and optimizing your campaigns, you can achieve significant results on LinkedIn. In the next sections, we will delve into more advanced tactics and strategies to further enhance your LinkedIn advertising efforts and drive business success.

4.3 Targeting Options and Best Practices

Effective targeting is crucial for the success of your LinkedIn advertising campaigns. LinkedIn offers a variety of targeting options that allow you to reach a specific audience based on their professional attributes and behaviors. This section explores the different targeting options available on LinkedIn and provides best practices for leveraging these options to maximize your campaign's impact.

Targeting Options on LinkedIn

LinkedIn's robust targeting capabilities enable you to narrow down your audience with precision. Here are the key targeting options:

1. Demographic Targeting

- **Location**: Target users based on their geographic location, such as country, state, city, or metropolitan area. This is essential for local marketing campaigns or when focusing on specific regions.
- **Age and Gender**: Refine your audience based on age and gender demographics.

2. Firmographic Targeting

- **Company**: Target specific companies by name or filter by company size, industry, and type (e.g., public, private, non-profit).

- **Company Connections**: Reach employees of companies that your company page admin or employees are connected with.

3. Job Experience Targeting

- **Job Title**: Target users based on their current job titles, ensuring your ads reach professionals in specific roles.
- **Job Function**: Focus on users based on their job functions, such as marketing, finance, or human resources.
- **Job Seniority**: Filter your audience by their level of seniority, from entry-level to C-suite executives.
- **Years of Experience**: Target users based on their overall professional experience.

4. Education Targeting

- **Schools**: Target alumni from specific universities or colleges.
- **Degrees**: Reach users based on their educational qualifications, such as bachelor's, master's, or doctoral degrees.
- **Fields of Study**: Narrow your audience by their field of study, relevant to specialized industries or roles.

5. Interest-Based Targeting

- **Groups**: Target members of specific LinkedIn groups related to your industry or interests.

- **Skills**: Focus on users with specific skills listed on their LinkedIn profiles.
- **Interests**: Target users based on their professional interests and activities on LinkedIn.

6. Custom Audiences

- **Website Retargeting**: Re-engage visitors who have previously interacted with your website.
- **Contact Targeting**: Upload a list of email addresses or contact information to target specific individuals.
- **Account-Based Targeting**: Target decision-makers and influencers at specific companies, ideal for B2B marketing.

Best Practices for Targeting on LinkedIn

To make the most of LinkedIn's targeting options, consider the following best practices:

1. Define Clear Audience Segments

Create detailed audience segments based on your campaign objectives. For instance, if you're promoting a leadership training program, segment your audience by job seniority and industry.

2. Combine Targeting Criteria

Use a combination of targeting options to narrow down your audience precisely. For example, target marketing managers in the technology industry located in North America. Combining criteria ensures your ads are shown to the most relevant audience.

3. Use Exclusions

Exclude irrelevant audiences to avoid wasting ad spend. For example, if you're targeting senior executives, you might exclude entry-level positions to refine your audience further.

4. Leverage Lookalike Audiences

Create lookalike audiences based on your existing high-value customers or leads. This helps you reach new users who share similar characteristics with your best-performing audience segments.

5. Utilize LinkedIn's Audience Expansion

Use LinkedIn's Audience Expansion feature to reach people similar to your target audience. This can help increase the reach of your campaigns while maintaining relevance.

6. Monitor and Adjust Targeting

Regularly review the performance of your targeting criteria. Use LinkedIn's analytics tools to identify which segments are performing well and which are underperforming. Adjust your targeting settings based on these insights to improve campaign effectiveness.

7. Test and Optimize

Conduct A/B tests with different targeting options to see what works best. Test various combinations of job titles, industries, and skills to find the optimal targeting strategy for your campaign.

8. Align Targeting with Ad Content

Ensure that your ad content is highly relevant to the audience you are targeting. Personalized and relevant ads are more likely to engage your audience and drive higher conversion rates.

Examples of Effective Targeting

Example 1: Promoting a Software Solution to IT Managers

- **Objective**: Generate leads for a new IT management software.
- **Targeting Criteria**:

- **Job Titles**: IT Manager, IT Director, Systems Administrator
  - **Industry**: Information Technology, Computer Software
  - **Location**: United States
  - **Skills**: Network Administration, IT Infrastructure, Cloud Computing

Example 2: Recruiting for a Marketing Position

- **Objective**: Attract qualified candidates for a marketing manager position.
- **Targeting Criteria**:

  - Job Titles: Marketing Manager, Digital Marketing Manager, Content Marketing Manager
  - Location: United Kingdom
  - Company Size: 50-200 employees
  - Years of Experience: 3-7 years

Example 3: Driving Registrations for a Webinar

- Objective: Increase registrations for a webinar on financial planning.
- Targeting Criteria:

  - Job Titles: Financial Advisor, Wealth Manager, Financial Planner
  - Industry: Financial Services, Banking

- Location: Canada
- Groups: Members of LinkedIn groups related to financial planning and investment

LinkedIn's extensive targeting options enable you to reach the most relevant audience for your marketing campaigns. By defining clear audience segments, combining targeting criteria, leveraging lookalike audiences, and continuously monitoring and optimizing your targeting strategy, you can enhance the effectiveness of your LinkedIn ads. In the next sections, we will delve into creating compelling ad content and optimizing your campaigns for the best possible results.

4.4 Creating Compelling Ad Creatives

Creating compelling ad creatives is essential for capturing your audience's attention and driving engagement on LinkedIn. A well-crafted ad can make the difference between a scroll and a click. This section outlines the key elements of effective ad creatives and provides best practices for designing ads that resonate with your target audience.

Key Elements of Effective Ad Creatives

Effective ad creatives consist of several crucial elements that work together to engage your audience and convey your message. These elements include:

1. Engaging Visuals

- **High-Quality Images**: Use high-resolution images that are relevant to your ad's message. Avoid using generic stock photos that don't add value.
- **Brand Consistency**: Ensure your visuals align with your brand's identity, using consistent colors, fonts, and styles.
- **Eye-Catching Design**: Create visually appealing designs that stand out in the LinkedIn feed. Use bold colors, clear layouts, and captivating graphics.

2. Compelling Headlines

- **Clear and Concise**: Your headline should be short, clear, and directly related to the value proposition of your ad.
- **Attention-grabbing**: Use action-oriented language and intriguing statements to draw in your audience.
- **Relevant**: Ensure your headline speaks directly to the needs or interests of your target audience.

3. Persuasive Ad Copy

- **Value Proposition**: Communicate the benefits of your product or service. Explain what makes it unique and why the audience should care.
- **Concise Messaging**: Keep your ad copy brief and to the point. LinkedIn users are typically busy professionals who appreciate straightforward messaging.

- **Audience-Focused**: Write from the perspective of your audience. Address their pain points, needs, and desires.

4. Strong Call to Action (CTA)

- **Clear Direction**: Tell your audience exactly what you want them to do next, such as "Learn More," "Download Now," "Register Today," or "Get Started."
- **Urgency**: Create a sense of urgency with phrases like "Limited Time Offer," "Sign Up Today," or "Don't Miss Out."
- **Visibility**: Make sure your CTA is prominent and easy to find within your ad creative.

Best Practices for Designing LinkedIn Ads

To create compelling LinkedIn ads that drive results, follow these best practices:

1. Understand Your Audience

- **Audience Insights**: Use LinkedIn's analytics and insights to understand your audience's demographics, interests, and behaviors.
- **Personalization**: Tailor your ad content to address the specific needs and preferences of your audience segments.

2. Use Professional Design Tools

- **Design Software**: Utilize professional design tools like Adobe Creative Cloud, Canva, or similar platforms to create high-quality visuals.
- **Templates**: Consider using LinkedIn's ad templates as a starting point, customizing them to fit your brand and message.

3. Test Different Creatives

- **A/B Testing**: Experiment with different images, headlines, ad copy, and CTAs to see what resonates best with your audience. Compare performance metrics to identify the most effective variations.
- **Iterative Improvements**: Use the insights gained from testing to continuously refine and improve your ad creatives.

4. Focus on Mobile Optimization

- **Mobile-Friendly Design**: Ensure your ad creatives are optimized for mobile devices. Use larger fonts, simple layouts, and images that look good on smaller screens.
- **Responsive Formats**: Choose ad formats that perform well across different devices, ensuring a seamless experience for all users.

5. Highlight Social Proof

- **Testimonials**: Include quotes or testimonials from satisfied customers to build credibility and trust.
- **Case Studies**: Share brief case studies or success stories that demonstrate the value of your product or service.
- **Endorsements**: Feature endorsements from reputable industry leaders or influencers to add authority to your message.

6. Keep It Fresh

- **Regular Updates**: Refresh your ad creatives regularly to prevent ad fatigue. Update images, headlines, and copy to keep your content fresh and engaging.
- **Seasonal Themes**: Incorporate seasonal or topical themes into your ads to make them more relevant and timely.

Examples of Compelling LinkedIn Ads

Example 1: Promoting a Webinar

- **Visual**: An engaging image of a speaker presenting at a previous event.
- **Headline**: "Join Our Free Webinar on Digital Marketing Trends!"
- **Ad Copy**: "Discover the latest strategies in digital marketing. Learn from industry experts and stay ahead of the curve. Limited spots available!"

- **CTA**: "Register Now"

Example 2: Advertising a Software Solution

- **Visual**: A screenshot of the software's dashboard with key features highlighted.
- **Headline**: "Transform Your Business with Our CRM Software"
- **Ad Copy**: "Streamline your sales process and improve customer relationships with our cutting-edge CRM solution. Try it free for 30 days."
- **CTA**: "Start Free Trial"

Example 3: Recruiting for a Job Opening

- **Visual**: A group photo of the company's team at work.
- **Headline**: "We're Hiring a Marketing Manager!"
- **Ad Copy**: "Join our dynamic team and help shape the future of marketing. Apply today to become part of an innovative and growing company."
- **CTA**: "Apply Now"

By focusing on engaging visuals, compelling headlines, persuasive ad copy, and strong calls to action, you can design ads that capture attention and drive meaningful engagement. Follow the best practices outlined in this section to optimize your ad creatives and achieve your LinkedIn advertising goals. In the next sections, we will explore advanced techniques for optimizing your campaigns and measuring their success.

4.5 Analyzing and Optimizing Ad Performance

Analyzing and optimizing the performance of your LinkedIn ads is crucial for ensuring the success of your campaigns. By regularly reviewing key metrics and making data-driven adjustments, you can enhance the effectiveness of your ads, maximize ROI, and achieve your marketing objectives. This section covers the essential steps and best practices for analyzing and optimizing your LinkedIn ad performance.

Key Metrics to Monitor

To evaluate the performance of your LinkedIn ads, focus on the following key metrics:

1. Impressions

- **Definition**: The number of times your ad is shown to users.
- **Significance**: High impressions indicate good visibility. However, it's important to consider engagement metrics alongside impressions to gauge the true impact.

2. Click-Through Rate (CTR)

- **Definition**: The percentage of users who click on your ad after seeing it.

- **Significance**: A higher CTR suggests that your ad is compelling and relevant to your audience. Calculate CTR by dividing the number of clicks by the number of impressions.

3. Cost Per Click (CPC)

- **Definition**: The average cost you pay for each click on your ad.
- **Significance**: CPC helps you understand the efficiency of your ad spend. A lower CPC indicates cost-effective engagement.

4. Conversion Rate

- **Definition**: The percentage of users who take the desired action (e.g., filling out a form, or making a purchase) after clicking your ad.
- **Significance**: A higher conversion rate indicates that your ad and landing page are effective in driving desired actions.

5. Cost Per Conversion

- **Definition**: The average cost you incur for each conversion.
- **Significance**: This metric helps you assess the profitability of your campaign. A lower cost per conversion signifies a more cost-effective campaign.

6. Engagement Metrics

- **Definition**: Metrics such as likes, shares, comments, and follows.
- **Significance**: High engagement rates indicate that your content resonates well with your audience and encourages interaction.

7. Return on Investment (ROI)

- **Definition**: The overall return generated from your ad spend.
- **Significance**: ROI measures the financial effectiveness of your campaign. Positive ROI means your campaign is profitable.

Best Practices for Analyzing Ad Performance

To effectively analyze your LinkedIn ad performance, follow these best practices:

1. Use LinkedIn Campaign Manager

- **Tool**: LinkedIn Campaign Manager provides detailed analytics and reporting tools to monitor your ad performance.
- **Features**: Track key metrics, generate performance reports, and visualize data trends.

2. Set Clear Benchmarks

- **Benchmarks**: Establish clear benchmarks and KPIs (Key Performance Indicators) before launching your campaign.
- **Comparison**: Use these benchmarks to compare actual performance and identify areas for improvement.

3. Segment Your Data

- **Segmentation**: Break down your data by different dimensions such as ad format, audience segment, location, and device.
- **Insight**: Segmenting your data helps identify which elements of your campaign are performing well and which need optimization.

4. Monitor Performance Regularly

- **Frequency**: Regularly check your campaign performance, ideally weekly or bi-weekly.
- **Trends**: Look for trends and patterns in your data to understand the long-term performance of your ads.

Optimization Techniques

Once you have analyzed your ad performance, use the following techniques to optimize your campaigns:

1. Refine Targeting

- **Audience Adjustments**: Use performance data to refine your targeting criteria. Focus on high-performing segments and exclude underperforming ones.
- **Lookalike Audiences**: Create lookalike audiences based on your best-performing segments to reach similar users.

2. A/B Testing

- **Variations**: Test different ad variations by changing one element at a time, such as headlines, images, or CTAs.
- **Comparison**: Compare the performance of each variation to determine the most effective elements.

3. Optimize Ad Creative

- **Engagement**: Use high-performing visuals and copy from successful ads in new campaigns.
- **Fresh Content**: Regularly update your ad creatives to avoid ad fatigue and keep your audience engaged.

4. Adjust Bidding Strategies

- **Bids**: Experiment with different bidding strategies, such as CPC or CPM, to find the most cost-effective approach.

- **Budget Allocation**: Allocate more budget to high-performing ads and reduce spend on low-performing ones.

5. Improve Landing Pages

- **Consistency**: Ensure your landing page matches the ad in terms of message and design.
- **Optimization**: Optimize your landing page for conversions by improving load speed, clarity, and user experience.

6. Leverage LinkedIn's Optimization Tools

- **Features**: Utilize LinkedIn's optimization tools, such as automated bidding and targeting recommendations, to enhance campaign performance.

Continuous Improvement

Optimization is an ongoing process. Continuously review and refine your campaigns based on the latest data and insights. Stay updated with LinkedIn's new features and best practices to keep your campaigns ahead of the competition.

By monitoring key metrics, using best practices for analysis, and implementing strategic optimization techniques, you can enhance your ad performance and achieve your marketing goals. In the next sections, we will explore advanced strategies for leveraging LinkedIn's features and tools to further boost your campaign success.

Chapter 5: Leveraging LinkedIn Analytics

LinkedIn Analytics is a powerful tool that provides in-depth insights into the performance of your content and advertising efforts. By leveraging LinkedIn Analytics, you can make informed decisions to optimize your marketing strategy, improve engagement, and drive better results. This chapter explores how to effectively use LinkedIn Analytics to gain valuable insights and enhance your marketing efforts.

Understanding LinkedIn Analytics

LinkedIn Analytics offers a comprehensive overview of how your LinkedIn Page, posts, and ads are performing. The main components of LinkedIn Analytics include:

1. Page Analytics

- **Visitor Analytics**: Provides data on the number of visitors to your LinkedIn Page, including metrics such as unique visitors, page views, and visitor demographics (e.g., job title, industry, location). This helps you understand who is visiting your page and tailor your content to attract the right audience.
- **Update Analytics**: Tracks the performance of your posts, including impressions, clicks, reactions, comments, shares, and engagement rate. This information helps you identify which types of content resonate most with your audience.
- **Follower Analytics**: Offers insights into your follower growth over time, including demographics and the source of your

followers (e.g., organic, sponsored). Understanding your follower base allows you to create content that appeals to them and fosters community growth.

2. Content and Engagement Analytics

- **Post-Performance**: Analyzes individual post performance to determine what content types (e.g., articles, images, and videos) generate the most engagement. You can use this data to replicate successful content and refine your content strategy.
- **Engagement Rate**: Measures the percentage of people who engage with your content out of those who see it. A high engagement rate indicates that your content is relevant and engaging to your audience.

3. Ad Analytics

- **Campaign Performance**: Provides detailed metrics on your LinkedIn ad campaigns, including impressions, clicks, CTR, conversions, and cost per conversion. These metrics help you assess the effectiveness of your ad campaigns and identify areas for improvement.
- **Audience Insights**: Offers data on the demographics and professional attributes of users who interact with your ads. This information helps you refine your targeting strategy and ensure your ads reach the right audience.

Leveraging LinkedIn Analytics for Optimization

To effectively leverage LinkedIn Analytics, follow these best practices:

1. Set Clear Goals and KPIs

Before diving into the data, establish clear goals and key performance indicators (KPIs) for your LinkedIn marketing efforts. Whether you aim to increase brand awareness, generate leads, or drive website traffic, having specific goals allows you to measure success and make data-driven decisions.

2. Regularly Monitor Performance

Consistently monitor your LinkedIn Analytics to track progress towards your goals. Regular analysis helps you identify trends, understand audience behavior, and make timely adjustments to your strategy. Set a routine to review your analytics weekly or monthly.

3. Analyze and Segment Your Audience

Use LinkedIn's demographic data to analyze and segment your audience based on factors such as job title, industry, and location. This segmentation helps you tailor your content and ads to the preferences and needs of different audience segments, improving engagement and conversion rates.

4. Optimize Content Strategy

Examine the performance of different types of content to identify what resonates most with your audience. For example, if video posts have higher engagement rates than text posts, consider incorporating more video content into your strategy. Continuously test and refine your content to keep it fresh and relevant.

5. Refine Ad Targeting

Use the insights gained from your ad analytics to refine your targeting strategy. If certain audience segments show higher engagement and conversion rates, focus more of your budget on these segments. Experiment with different targeting criteria to optimize ad performance.

6. A/B Test and Iterate

Conduct A/B tests to compare the performance of different ad variations, such as headlines, images, and CTAs. Use the results to identify the most effective elements and iterate on your ad creatives. Continuous testing and optimization are key to improving ad performance.

7. Measure ROI

Evaluate the return on investment (ROI) of your LinkedIn marketing efforts by comparing the cost of your campaigns to the revenue generated. This analysis helps you determine the financial impact of your LinkedIn activities and allocate your budget more effectively.

Leveraging LinkedIn Analytics is essential for optimizing your marketing strategy and achieving your business objectives. By regularly monitoring performance, analyzing audience insights, and continuously refining your content and ad strategies, you can enhance your LinkedIn presence and drive better results. In the following chapters, we will explore advanced techniques and strategies to further leverage LinkedIn's features and tools for maximum impact.

5.1 Overview of LinkedIn Analytics Tools

LinkedIn Analytics is an essential resource for businesses and marketers aiming to optimize their presence on the platform. It provides a wealth of data and insights that can help you understand how your content and campaigns are performing, who your audience is, and how to better engage with them. This section provides an in-depth overview of the key LinkedIn Analytics tools available and how they can be leveraged to enhance your marketing strategy.

LinkedIn Page Analytics

LinkedIn Page Analytics offers a comprehensive view of how your company page is performing. It includes several key areas:

Visitor Analytics

Visitor analytics help you understand who is visiting your LinkedIn Page. The main metrics include:

- **Unique Visitors**: The number of individual users who visited your page.
- **Page Views**: The total number of times your page was viewed.
- **Visitor Demographics**: Detailed insights into the professional attributes of your visitors, such as job title, industry, location, and company size.

These metrics allow you to gauge the reach and attractiveness of your LinkedIn Page, helping you tailor your content to better meet the interests and needs of your visitors.

Update Analytics

Update analytics provide data on the performance of your posts. Key metrics include:

- **Impressions**: The number of times your post was seen by users.
- **Clicks**: The number of times users clicked on your post.
- **Reactions**, **Comments**, **and Shares**: The engagement metrics that show how users are interacting with your content.
- **Engagement Rate**: The percentage of users who engaged with your post out of the total number of impressions.

By analyzing these metrics, you can identify which types of content are most engaging for your audience and refine your content strategy accordingly.

Follower Analytics

Follower analytics offer insights into the growth and demographics of your followers:

- **Follower Growth**: Tracks the increase or decrease in the number of followers over time.
- **Follower Demographics**: Provides detailed information on the professional attributes of your followers, such as seniority, job function, and geographic location.

Understanding your follower base helps you create content that resonates with them and attracts more followers who fit your target audience profile.

LinkedIn Content and Engagement Analytics

LinkedIn's content and engagement analytics provide a deeper dive into how individual pieces of content are performing. This includes:

- **Post-Performance**: Detailed metrics on individual posts, including impressions, clicks, engagement, and shares. This helps you understand what type of content works best.
- **Engagement Metrics**: Includes likes, comments, and shares. High engagement rates indicate that your content is resonating with your audience and encouraging interaction.

These insights are critical for fine-tuning your content strategy and ensuring you are delivering valuable and engaging content to your audience.

LinkedIn Ad Analytics

LinkedIn Ad Analytics provides a detailed overview of your ad campaigns' performance, allowing you to optimize your advertising efforts. Key areas include:

Campaign Performance

- **Impressions**: The number of times your ads were shown.
- **Clicks and CTR**: The number of clicks your ads received and the click-through rate.
- **Conversions**: The number of desired actions taken by users, such as filling out a form or making a purchase.
- **Cost Metrics**: Including cost per click (CPC) and cost per conversion, which help you assess the efficiency of your ad spend.

These metrics allow you to evaluate the effectiveness of your ad campaigns and make data-driven decisions to improve their performance.

Audience Insights

- **Demographics**: Information on the professional attributes of users who interacted with your ads, such as job title, industry, and company size.
- **Engagement Insights**: Data on how different segments of your audience are engaging with your ads.

By understanding who is engaging with your ads, you can refine your targeting strategies to reach the most relevant audience.

LinkedIn Analytics Tools in Practice

To effectively leverage LinkedIn Analytics, you should:

- **Regularly Monitor Performance**: Keep track of your key metrics to stay informed about how your content and campaigns are performing.
- **Set Clear Goals**: Establish benchmarks and KPIs to measure your success.
- **Segment Your Data**: Break down your analytics data to gain insights into specific audience segments.

- **Optimize Content and Ads**: Use the insights gained to refine your content strategy and ad targeting.

LinkedIn Analytics provides invaluable insights that can help you optimize your marketing strategy, engage your audience more effectively, and achieve your business objectives. By regularly monitoring and analyzing your LinkedIn data, you can make informed decisions that drive better results on the platform. In the following sections, we will explore more advanced techniques and strategies for leveraging LinkedIn's analytics tools to maximize your marketing impact.

5.2 Measuring Key Metrics and KPIs

Measuring key metrics and Key Performance Indicators (KPIs) is crucial for evaluating the success of your LinkedIn marketing efforts. Understanding these metrics allows you to assess the effectiveness of your campaigns, optimize your strategy, and achieve your business goals. This section delves into the most important metrics and KPIs you should track on LinkedIn, how to interpret them, and how to use them to drive continuous improvement.

Key Metrics and KPIs for LinkedIn Marketing

1. **Impressions**

- **Definition**: The number of times your content is displayed to LinkedIn users.

- **Importance**: High impressions indicate good visibility. However, impressions alone don't measure engagement or effectiveness. They should be analyzed alongside engagement metrics to understand the true impact.

2. Click-Through Rate (CTR)

- **Definition**: The percentage of impressions that result in clicks.
- **Calculation**: CTR = (Clicks / Impressions) x 100.
- **Importance**: A higher CTR indicates that your content or ads are compelling and relevant to your audience. It's a critical measure of how effectively your headlines, visuals, and overall messaging attract attention.

3. Engagement Rate

- **Definition**: The percentage of users who engage with your content (e.g., likes, comments, shares) out of the total impressions.
- **Calculation**: Engagement Rate = (Total Engagements / Impressions) x 100.
- **Importance**: High engagement rates show that your content resonates with your audience and encourages interaction. It's a key indicator of content effectiveness and audience engagement.

4. Conversion Rate

- **Definition**: The percentage of users who take the desired action after clicking your ad or content (e.g., filling out a form, or making a purchase).
- **Calculation**: Conversion Rate = (Conversions / Clicks) x 100.
- **Importance**: A higher conversion rate indicates that your content and landing pages are effective at driving the desired actions. It's a critical metric for measuring the success of lead generation and sales campaigns.

5. Cost Per Click (CPC)

- **Definition**: The average cost you pay for each click on your ad.
- **Calculation**: CPC = Total Spend / Total Clicks.
- **Importance**: CPC helps you understand the efficiency of your ad spend. Lower CPC means more cost-effective traffic and engagement.

6. Cost Per Conversion (CPA)

- **Definition**: The average cost to acquire a conversion.
- **Calculation**: CPA = Total Spend / Total Conversions.
- **Importance**: CPA measures the cost-effectiveness of your campaigns in generating desired actions. A lower CPA indicates more efficient use of your marketing budget.

7. Return on Investment (ROI)

- **Definition**: The overall return generated from your marketing efforts relative to the cost.
- **Calculation**: ROI = (Revenue - Cost) / Cost x 100.
- **Importance**: ROI measures the financial effectiveness of your marketing campaigns. Positive ROI indicates that your campaigns are profitable.

How to Measure and Use These Metrics

Step 1: Set Clear Objectives

Before tracking metrics, establish clear objectives for your LinkedIn marketing efforts. Objectives might include increasing brand awareness, generating leads, driving website traffic, or boosting sales. Clear goals provide a benchmark for measuring success.

Step 2: Use LinkedIn Analytics Tools

Leverage LinkedIn's analytics tools, such as LinkedIn Page Analytics and Campaign Manager, to gather data on your key metrics. Regularly monitor these tools to stay informed about your performance.

Step 3: Analyze and Interpret Data

- **Trends**: Look for trends and patterns over time. Are there specific times or days when your content performs better?
- **Comparisons**: Compare different types of content or ad formats to see which ones perform best.
- **Segments**: Analyze performance across different audience segments to understand who is most engaged with your content.

Step 4: Make Data-Driven Decisions

Use the insights gained from your analysis to make informed decisions about your marketing strategy. For example:

- If your CTR is low, consider refining your headlines or visuals to make them more compelling.
- If your engagement rate is high but the conversion rate is low, evaluate your landing page and call-to-action to ensure they are clear and persuasive.
- If your CPA is high, explore ways to optimize your ad targeting to reach a more relevant audience.

Step 5: Continuous Optimization

Optimization is an ongoing process. Regularly review your metrics and KPIs to identify areas for improvement. Implement changes, track their impact, and iterate based on the results. Continuous optimization helps you refine your strategy and achieve better outcomes over time.

Measuring key metrics and KPIs is essential for evaluating and optimizing your LinkedIn marketing efforts. By understanding and tracking metrics such as impressions, CTR, engagement rate, conversion rate, CPC, CPA, and ROI, you can gain valuable insights into the performance of your campaigns. Use these insights to make data-driven decisions, continuously optimize your strategy, and achieve your marketing objectives. In the next sections, we will explore advanced techniques for leveraging LinkedIn Analytics to maximize your marketing impact.

5.3 Using Analytics to Refine Your Strategy

Leveraging LinkedIn Analytics to refine your marketing strategy is essential for continuous improvement and achieving better results. By interpreting data and making informed adjustments, you can enhance your content, optimize ad campaigns, and engage more effectively with your audience. This section outlines how to use LinkedIn Analytics to refine your strategy, including practical steps and examples.

Step 1: Regularly Review Your Analytics

Establish a routine for reviewing your LinkedIn Analytics. Weekly or monthly check-ins allow you to stay updated on performance trends and make timely adjustments. Focus on key metrics such as impressions, engagement rates, click-through rates (CTR), and conversion rates to understand how your content and ads are performing.

Step 2: Identify High-Performing Content

Analyze which types of content generate the most engagement. Look at metrics such as likes, comments, shares, and CTR. Identify patterns in high-performing posts. For example, if video content consistently receives higher engagement than text posts, consider incorporating more videos into your content strategy.

Step 3: Evaluate Audience Engagement

Use demographic data and engagement insights to understand your audience better. LinkedIn provides information on job titles, industries, locations, and seniority levels of your followers and visitors. Tailor your content to meet the preferences and interests of your audience segments. For instance, if a significant portion of your audience is in the technology sector, create content that addresses trends and challenges in that industry.

Step 4: Optimize Ad Campaigns

Examine the performance of your LinkedIn ad campaigns by reviewing metrics such as CPC, CPA, and conversion rates. Identify which ads perform best and why. Adjust your targeting criteria to focus on high-performing audience segments. If your ads targeting senior executives have a higher conversion rate, allocate more budget to that segment. Conduct A/B tests to compare different ad variations and refine your creatives based on the results.

Step 5: Improve Landing Pages

High conversion rates on LinkedIn ads but low follow-through on landing pages can indicate issues with the landing page experience. Use analytics to pinpoint where users drop off and optimize your landing pages accordingly. Ensure consistency between your ad messaging and landing page content. Improve the clarity and persuasiveness of your call-to-action (CTA) and reduce any friction points that might deter conversions.

Step 6: Adjust Posting Schedules

Analyze the times and days when your audience is most active. LinkedIn Analytics can show you when your posts receive the most engagement. Schedule your posts during these peak times to maximize visibility and interaction. Experiment with different posting schedules and monitor the impact on engagement metrics to find the optimal times for your audience.

Step 7: Monitor Competitor Performance

LinkedIn Analytics can also help you gain insights into your competitors' performance. Observe their content strategies, engagement rates, and follower growth. Identify what works for them and consider incorporating similar tactics into your strategy. However, ensure your content remains unique and aligned with your brand's voice and values.

Step 8: Set and Reevaluate Goals

Use your analytics data to set realistic, data-driven goals. If your initial goal was to increase engagement by 20% in six months, track your progress and adjust your tactics as needed. Regularly reevaluate your goals based on your performance data and industry trends. Ensure your objectives are specific, measurable, achievable, relevant, and time-bound (SMART).

Example Scenario

Imagine your LinkedIn Page has seen a steady increase in impressions but a decline in engagement rates. By reviewing your analytics, you notice that posts featuring infographics and industry insights receive higher engagement than promotional content. In response, you decide to:

- Increase the frequency of infographic posts.
- Share more industry insights and thought leadership articles.
- Reduce the number of purely promotional posts.

You also observe that your audience is most active on weekdays between 9 AM and 11 AM. You adjust your posting schedule to align with these peak times. Over the next month, you monitor the impact of these changes, noting a significant increase in engagement rates and improved audience interaction.

Using LinkedIn Analytics to refine your strategy is a dynamic and ongoing process. Regularly reviewing your analytics, identifying high-performing content, optimizing ad campaigns, and tailoring your approach based on audience insights are crucial steps in enhancing your LinkedIn marketing efforts. By making data-driven adjustments and continuously experimenting, you can achieve better engagement, higher conversion rates, and ultimately, more successful marketing outcomes. In the following sections, we will delve into advanced techniques for leveraging LinkedIn's features and tools to maximize your marketing impact.

5.4 Reporting and Presenting Your Results

Effectively reporting and presenting your LinkedIn marketing results is crucial for demonstrating the value of your efforts to stakeholders and for guiding future strategy. Clear, concise, and insightful reports help you communicate key findings, showcase successes, and identify areas for improvement. This section outlines best practices for creating impactful reports and presentations that highlight your LinkedIn marketing performance.

Step 1: Define Your Audience

Understanding who will be reading or viewing your report is the first step. Tailor your report to meet the needs and interests of your audience, whether they are executives, marketing teams, or clients. Different stakeholders may require different levels of detail and types of insights.

Step 2: Set Clear Objectives

Clarify the purpose of your report. Are you showcasing the success of a particular campaign, providing a monthly performance overview, or presenting quarterly results? Having a clear objective helps you focus on the most relevant data and insights.

Step 3: Choose Key Metrics and KPIs

Select the most important metrics and KPIs to include in your report. Common LinkedIn metrics to report on include:

- **Impressions**: Indicates the reach of your content.
- **Engagement Rate**: This shows how well your content resonates with your audience.
- **Click-Through Rate (CTR)**: Measures the effectiveness of your content in driving traffic.
- **Conversion Rate**: Indicates how well your content or ads are driving desired actions.
- **Cost Per Click (CPC) and Cost Per Acquisition (CPA)**: Important for assessing the efficiency of your ad spend.
- **Follower Growth**: Reflects the growth of your LinkedIn audience.

Step 4: Use Visuals for Clarity

Visual representations of data, such as charts, graphs, and infographics, make complex information easier to understand. Use visuals to highlight key trends and comparisons. For example, a line graph showing follower growth over time can quickly convey how your audience is expanding.

Step 5: Provide Context

Data alone doesn't tell the whole story. Provide context to help your audience understand what the numbers mean. Explain any significant changes or trends, such as why engagement spiked during a specific campaign or why CTR dropped for a particular ad. Contextual insights make your report more informative and actionable.

Step 6: Highlight Key Insights and Actions

Identify the most important insights from your data and highlight them in your report. What worked well? What didn't? What are the key takeaways? Based on these insights, recommend actionable steps to improve future performance. For example, if video posts had higher engagement rates, suggest incorporating more video content into your strategy.

Step 7: Structure Your Report

Organize your report in a logical and coherent structure. A typical structure might include:

- **Executive Summary**: A brief overview of the key findings and outcomes.
- **Objectives**: The goals of your LinkedIn marketing efforts.
- **Performance Overview**: A summary of key metrics and KPIs.

- **Detailed Analysis**: In-depth analysis of specific campaigns, content types, or audience segments.
- **Key Insights**: Highlighted findings and their implications.
- **Recommendations**: Suggested actions based on the insights.
- **Conclusion**: A wrap-up of the report with final thoughts and next steps.

Step 8: Tailor Your Presentation Style

When presenting your report, tailor your style to your audience. For executives, focus on high-level insights and strategic implications. For marketing teams, dive deeper into the data and discuss specific tactics and performance details. Use a clear and engaging presentation format, such as PowerPoint or a digital dashboard, to make your findings accessible and easy to understand.

Example Scenario

Imagine you're reporting on a LinkedIn marketing campaign aimed at increasing brand awareness and generating leads. Your report might include:

- **Executive Summary**: "This report highlights the success of our Q2 LinkedIn marketing campaign, which increased brand awareness and generated a significant number of leads."
- **Objectives**: "The campaign aimed to increase impressions by 20%, boost engagement by 15%, and generate 100 qualified leads."

- **Performance Overview**: Use visuals to show that impressions increased by 25%, engagement by 18%, and 120 qualified leads were generated.
- **Detailed Analysis**: Break down the performance of different types of content, showing that video posts had the highest engagement rates and that ads targeting senior professionals had the highest conversion rates.
- **Key Insights**: "Video content and targeted ads were the most effective strategies."
- **Recommendations**: "Increase the use of video content in future campaigns and continue targeting senior professionals for lead generation."
- **Conclusion**: Summarize the success of the campaign and outline the next steps, such as implementing the recommended actions.

Effective reporting and presentation of your LinkedIn marketing results are essential for demonstrating the value of your efforts and guiding future strategies. By clearly defining your audience, setting objectives, selecting key metrics, using visuals, providing context, highlighting insights, structuring your report logically, and tailoring your presentation style, you can create impactful reports that drive informed decision-making and continuous improvement. In the next sections, we will explore more advanced techniques for leveraging LinkedIn's analytics tools to maximize your marketing impact.

5.5 Case Studies of Successful LinkedIn Analytics Use

Case studies provide valuable insights into how different organizations have successfully leveraged LinkedIn Analytics to optimize their marketing strategies and achieve their business goals. In this section, we will explore several case studies that highlight the practical application of LinkedIn Analytics in driving success.

Case Study 1: TechCorp - Boosting Engagement Through Content Optimization

Background:

TechCorp, a B2B technology solutions provider, aimed to increase engagement on their LinkedIn company page. Despite a steady flow of content, they noticed low engagement rates.

Strategy:

TechCorp used LinkedIn Analytics to analyze the performance of their posts over three months. They identified the types of content that received the highest engagement, such as industry news, how-to guides, and customer success stories.

Actions:

- **Content Audit**: TechCorp conducted a content audit using analytics to categorize posts by type and engagement rate.
- **Content Focus**: They shifted their content strategy to focus on high-performing content types, particularly how-to guides and success stories.

- **Posting Schedule**: By analyzing the times when their audience was most active, they adjusted their posting schedule to align with peak engagement hours.

Results:

- **Engagement Rate**: Increased by 35% within two months.
- **Followers**: Grew by 20% as a result of more engaging and relevant content.
- **Brand Visibility**: Enhanced visibility in the technology sector, leading to increased inquiries and potential leads.

Case Study 2: HealthCarePlus - Improving Ad Performance with Targeted Campaigns

Background:

HealthCarePlus, a healthcare services provider, wanted to improve the performance of their LinkedIn ad campaigns aimed at generating leads for their new telehealth services.

Strategy:

Using LinkedIn Ad Analytics, HealthCarePlus reviewed the performance of their ad campaigns to understand which ads and audience segments were most effective.

Actions:

- **Audience Segmentation**: They identified that ads targeting healthcare professionals and administrators had higher conversion rates.
- **Ad Creatives**: HealthCarePlus optimized its ad creatives by focusing on clear, concise messaging that highlighted the benefits of its telehealth services.
- **A/B Testing**: Implemented A/B testing to compare different ad variations and determine the most effective combinations of visuals and copy.

Results:

- **Conversion Rate**: Increased by 50%, leading to a significant rise in telehealth service inquiries.
- **Cost Per Acquisition (CPA)**: Reduced by 30%, making their ad spending more efficient.
- **Lead Quality**: Improved lead quality, with a higher percentage of leads converting into actual customers.

Case Study 3: GreenEnergy Solutions - Expanding Market Reach with Data-Driven Insights

Background:

GreenEnergy Solutions, a renewable energy company, aimed to expand its market reach and increase brand awareness among industry professionals and potential clients.

Strategy:

GreenEnergy Solutions utilized LinkedIn Analytics to gain insights into their audience demographics and engagement patterns. They focused on understanding which content resonated most with their target audience.

Actions:

- **Demographic Analysis**: Leveraged visitor demographics to tailor content to specific audience segments, such as sustainability officers and environmental engineers.
- **Content Diversification**: Expanded their content strategy to include more case studies, industry reports, and infographics that highlighted the impact of renewable energy solutions.
- **Engagement Tracking**: Monitored engagement metrics to continuously refine their content and posting strategy.

Results:

- **Impressions**: Increased by 40%, reaching a wider audience within the renewable energy sector.
- **Engagement**: Grew by 25%, with more likes, comments, and shares on their posts.

- **Market Reach**: Successfully expanded their market reach, leading to new business opportunities and partnerships.

Case Study 4: EduFuture - Enhancing Educational Program Enrollment

Background:

EduFuture, an online education platform, aimed to boost enrollment for their new certification programs through LinkedIn marketing.

Strategy:

EduFuture used LinkedIn Analytics to track the effectiveness of their posts and ads in driving traffic to their program landing pages.

Actions:

- **Performance Analysis**: Reviewed the performance of different content types to identify what drove the most traffic and conversions.
- **Targeted Ads**: Created targeted ad campaigns focusing on professionals seeking career advancement in specific industries.
- **Landing Page Optimization**: Improved their landing pages based on analytics insights, ensuring a seamless user experience that encouraged conversions.

Results:

- **Enrollment Rates**: Increased by 45%, with more users signing up for certification programs.
- **Website Traffic**: Boosted by 60%, as a result of more effective content and ad strategies.
- **Return on Investment (ROI)**: Achieved a higher ROI on their LinkedIn marketing spend, proving the effectiveness of their data-driven approach.

These case studies demonstrate the power of LinkedIn Analytics in refining marketing strategies and achieving business goals. By understanding and leveraging key metrics, organizations can optimize their content, improve ad performance, expand their reach, and ultimately drive better results. In the following sections, we will explore advanced techniques for leveraging LinkedIn's analytics tools to maximize your marketing impact further.

Chapter 6: Advanced LinkedIn Marketing Tactics

As you become more familiar with LinkedIn's basic features and analytics, it's time to explore advanced tactics that can elevate your marketing efforts. These strategies will help you maximize your reach, engage with your audience on a deeper level, and drive conversions more effectively. In this chapter, we will delve into sophisticated LinkedIn marketing techniques that can give you a competitive edge.

1. Utilizing LinkedIn Sales Navigator

LinkedIn Sales Navigator is a powerful tool designed to help businesses find and build relationships with prospects. This advanced tool provides enhanced search capabilities, personalized algorithms, and actionable insights.

Key Features:

- **Advanced Search**: Use detailed filters to find leads and accounts that match your ideal customer profile.
- **Lead Recommendations**: Get suggestions for potential leads based on your preferences and activities.
- **InMail Messages**: Send direct messages to prospects, even if you're not connected.
- **CRM Integration**: Sync with your CRM to streamline your sales process.

Implementation:

- **Define Your Target Audience**: Use Sales Navigator to create a detailed profile of your ideal customer.
- **Search and Save Leads**: Use advanced search filters to find potential leads and save them for follow-up.
- **Engage with InMail**: Craft personalized messages to initiate conversations with prospects.
- **Track and Analyze**: Monitor interactions and adjust your approach based on engagement metrics.

2. Leveraging LinkedIn Live for Real-Time Engagement

LinkedIn Live allows you to broadcast live video content to your network, fostering real-time interaction and engagement. This feature is ideal for product launches, Q&A sessions, webinars, and virtual events.

Benefits:

- **Increased Engagement**: Live videos tend to generate more engagement than pre-recorded content.
- **Real-Time Interaction**: Engage with your audience directly through comments and reactions.
- **Enhanced Visibility**: LinkedIn promotes live broadcasts, increasing their reach.

Best Practices:

- **Plan Your Content**: Define the purpose of your live broadcast and outline the key points you want to cover.
- **Promote Your Event**: Announce your live session in advance to build anticipation and ensure a larger audience.
- **Engage Actively**: Interact with viewers by responding to comments and questions in real-time.
- **Analyze Performance**: After the broadcast, review the analytics to understand viewer behavior and improve future sessions.

3. Implementing LinkedIn Retargeting Campaigns

Retargeting on LinkedIn allows you to reach users who have previously interacted with your brand, increasing the likelihood of conversion. This tactic involves showing ads to people who have visited your website or engaged with your LinkedIn content.

Steps to Set Up Retargeting:

- **Install the LinkedIn Insight Tag**: Add this tracking code to your website to gather data on visitors.
- **Create Retargeting Audiences**: Segment visitors based on their behavior, such as pages visited or actions taken.
- **Develop Targeted Ads**: Craft ads tailored to the interests and needs of your retargeting audience.
- **Monitor and Optimize**: Track the performance of your retargeting campaigns and make adjustments to improve results.

4. Harnessing LinkedIn Sponsored Content

LinkedIn Sponsored Content allows you to promote your posts to a broader audience beyond your followers. This form of native advertising can increase visibility, engagement, and lead generation.

Tips for Effective Sponsored Content:

- **Create Compelling Content**: Ensure your content is relevant, informative, and visually appealing.
- **Target Precisely**: Use LinkedIn's robust targeting options to reach your ideal audience based on demographics, job titles, industries, and more.
- **Test and Iterate**: Experiment with different types of sponsored content and refine your approach based on performance data.
- **Measure Impact**: Use LinkedIn Analytics to track the success of your sponsored content and adjust your strategy accordingly.

5. Engaging with LinkedIn Influencers

Collaborating with LinkedIn influencers can amplify your brand's message and reach a larger, more engaged audience. Influencers can help build credibility and trust for your brand through authentic endorsements.

Steps to Engage with Influencers:

- **Identify Relevant Influencers**: Use LinkedIn to find influencers who align with your brand values and target audience.
- **Build Relationships**: Engage with influencers by commenting on their posts, sharing their content, and initiating conversations.
- **Collaborate on Content**: Partner with influencers to create co-branded content, such as blog posts, videos, or webinars.
- **Leverage Influencer Networks**: Encourage influencers to share your content with their followers to expand your reach.

6. Utilizing LinkedIn Analytics for Continuous Improvement

Advanced use of LinkedIn Analytics involves not just tracking metrics but also using data to refine and enhance your marketing strategy continuously.

Advanced Analytics Techniques:

- **Segmentation Analysis**: Break down your audience into segments to understand how different groups interact with your content.
- **A/B Testing**: Experiment with different versions of ads and content to determine what resonates best with your audience.
- **Conversion Tracking**: Set up conversion tracking to measure the ROI of your LinkedIn campaigns accurately.
- **Benchmarking**: Compare your performance against industry benchmarks to identify areas for improvement.

Advanced LinkedIn marketing tactics require a strategic approach, leveraging sophisticated tools and features to enhance your reach and engagement. By utilizing LinkedIn Sales Navigator, LinkedIn Live, retargeting campaigns, sponsored content, influencer collaborations, and advanced analytics, you can optimize your LinkedIn marketing strategy and achieve greater success. In the next chapter, we will explore how to integrate LinkedIn with other marketing channels to create a cohesive and effective marketing ecosystem.

6.1 LinkedIn Sales Navigator and Lead Generation

LinkedIn Sales Navigator is a premium tool designed to help businesses find and build relationships with prospects, making it an essential asset for lead generation. With its advanced search capabilities, personalized algorithms, and actionable insights, Sales Navigator transforms LinkedIn into a powerful lead generation engine. In this section, we'll explore how to effectively use LinkedIn Sales Navigator to generate high-quality leads.

Understanding LinkedIn Sales Navigator

LinkedIn Sales Navigator offers several features that streamline the process of finding and engaging with potential leads:

- **Advanced Search and Filters**: Sales Navigator allows you to conduct highly specific searches using a wide range of filters, including job titles, company size, industry, geography, and more.

This precision helps you identify prospects who closely match your ideal customer profile.

- **Lead Recommendations**: The tool provides personalized lead recommendations based on your preferences and past activities, helping you discover new prospects you might not have found otherwise.
- **InMail Messaging**: With Sales Navigator, you can send direct messages, known as InMails, to any LinkedIn user, even if you're not connected. This feature enables you to reach out to potential leads directly and initiate conversations.
- **CRM Integration**: Sales Navigator can integrate with your existing Customer Relationship Management (CRM) system, allowing you to sync data and streamline your sales processes.
- **TeamLink**: This feature shows you connections within your network who can introduce you to potential leads, leveraging the power of mutual connections to build trust and facilitate introductions.

Implementing LinkedIn Sales Navigator for Lead Generation

Step 1: Define Your Ideal Customer Profile

The first step in leveraging Sales Navigator for lead generation is to clearly define your ideal customer profile. Consider factors such as:

- **Industry**: Identify the industries where your product or service is most applicable.
- **Company Size**: Determine whether you are targeting small businesses, mid-sized companies, or large enterprises.

- **Job Titles**: Specify the roles and decision-makers who are most likely to benefit from your offerings.
- **Geographic Location**: Focus on regions where you can serve customers effectively.

Step 2: Conduct Advanced Searches

Use the advanced search feature to find prospects that match your ideal customer profile. Apply relevant filters to narrow down your search and generate a list of high-quality leads. Save these leads within Sales Navigator to keep track of your prospects and manage your pipeline efficiently.

Step 3: Engage with Personalized InMail

Craft personalized InMail messages to reach out to your leads. Personalization is key to standing out and making a positive impression. Mention specific details about the prospect's background or company to show that you've done your research. Highlight how your product or service can address their specific needs or pain points.

Step 4: Leverage Lead Recommendations

Regularly review the lead recommendations provided by Sales Navigator. These suggestions are tailored based on your previous interactions and search criteria, offering a continuous stream of potential prospects.

Step 5: Utilize CRM Integration

Integrate Sales Navigator with your CRM to keep your lead data organized and up-to-date. This integration ensures that your sales and marketing teams have access to the same information, facilitating better collaboration and more effective follow-up.

Step 6: Monitor and Adjust Your Approach

Track the performance of your outreach efforts using the insights provided by Sales Navigator. Monitor response rates, engagement levels, and conversion rates to identify what works best. Use this data to refine your messaging, targeting, and overall lead-generation strategy.

Example Scenario

Imagine a software company, TechInnovate, specializing in cybersecurity solutions for mid-sized enterprises. They use LinkedIn Sales Navigator to identify potential leads among IT managers and security officers in the financial services industry. By applying filters for industry, job title, and company size, TechInnovate generates a targeted list of prospects.

The sales team then sends personalized InMail messages to these leads, highlighting how their cybersecurity solution addresses specific industry challenges. They track engagement through Sales Navigator and their CRM, refining their approach based on response data. As a result, TechInnovate sees a significant increase in high-quality leads and ultimately, more conversions.

LinkedIn Sales Navigator is a robust tool that, when used effectively, can significantly enhance your lead generation efforts. By defining your ideal customer profile, utilizing advanced search and filters, engaging with personalized InMail, leveraging lead recommendations, integrating with your CRM, and continuously monitoring your approach, you can build a steady pipeline of high-quality leads. In the following sections, we will explore more advanced tactics to further optimize your LinkedIn marketing strategy.

6.2 Using LinkedIn for Thought Leadership

Establishing thought leadership on LinkedIn is a powerful way to enhance your brand's credibility, attract a loyal audience, and position yourself or your company as an authority in your industry. LinkedIn provides various tools and opportunities to share insights, engage with professionals, and build a reputation as a thought leader. This section explores how to effectively use LinkedIn to develop and showcase thought leadership.

Understanding Thought Leadership

Thought leadership involves sharing valuable insights, expertise, and perspectives that influence your industry and guide others. Thought leaders are recognized for their deep knowledge, innovative ideas, and ability to address complex challenges. On LinkedIn, thought leadership can be demonstrated through various types of content, interactions, and engagements.

Steps to Establish Thought Leadership on LinkedIn

Step 1: Define Your Niche and Audience

Begin by identifying your specific area of expertise and the audience you want to reach. Consider the following:

- **Niche**: Focus on a particular field or topic where you have deep knowledge and can provide unique insights.
- **Audience**: Determine who will benefit most from your content, such as industry professionals, potential clients, or peers.

Understanding your niche and audience helps tailor your content and messaging to resonate with the right people.

Step 2: Optimize Your Profile

Your LinkedIn profile is your digital business card. Ensure it reflects your expertise and thought leadership:

- **Headline**: Craft a compelling headline that highlights your expertise and value proposition.
- **Summary**: Write a concise summary that showcases your background, achievements, and thought leadership focus.
- **Experience**: Detail your professional experience, emphasizing roles and accomplishments that reinforce your expertise.

- **Skills and Endorsements**: Highlight relevant skills and seek endorsements from colleagues and industry peers.
- **Recommendations**: Request recommendations from respected professionals who can vouch for your expertise and thought leadership.

Step 3: Create High-Quality Content

Consistently sharing high-quality content is crucial for building thought leadership. Focus on the following types of content:

- **Articles**: Write long-form articles on LinkedIn to delve into complex topics, share research findings, or offer in-depth analysis. Articles demonstrate your expertise and provide substantial value to your audience.
- **Posts**: Share regular updates, insights, and shorter pieces of content. Use posts to discuss industry trends, share quick tips, or comment on relevant news.
- **Videos**: Create videos to share your thoughts, conduct interviews with industry experts, or present at virtual events. Videos are engaging and help humanize your brand.
- **Infographics and Slides**: Use visual content to present data, research findings, or process explanations in an easy-to-digest format.

Step 4: Engage with Your Network

Active engagement with your LinkedIn network is essential for building thought leadership:

- **Comment on Posts**: Provide thoughtful comments on posts from others in your industry. Engaging in discussions shows your active involvement and insight.
- **Respond to Comments**: Encourage conversations on your posts by responding to comments. This interaction builds relationships and demonstrates your willingness to engage.
- **Join Groups**: Participate in LinkedIn Groups relevant to your industry. Share your insights, answer questions, and contribute to discussions.
- **Follow Influencers**: Follow other thought leaders in your field. Engage with their content and build relationships with them.

Step 5: Collaborate with Influencers

Collaborating with established influencers can amplify your thought leadership efforts:

- **Guest Posts**: Write guest articles for influential industry blogs or publications. This expands your reach and credibility.
- **Interviews**: Conduct interviews with industry experts and share them on LinkedIn. This association enhances your authority and provides valuable content for your audience.
- **Webinars and Panels**: Participate in webinars, panels, and virtual events as a speaker or moderator. These opportunities allow you to share your expertise with a broader audience.

Step 6: Analyze and Refine Your Strategy

Regularly review the performance of your thought leadership efforts to understand what resonates with your audience:

- **Engagement Metrics**: Monitor likes, comments, shares, and views on your content to gauge engagement.
- **Feedback**: Pay attention to feedback from your audience. Adjust your content strategy based on what they find valuable.
- **Content Performance**: Analyze which types of content perform best and focus on creating more of that content.

Example Scenario

Imagine Sarah, a cybersecurity expert, wants to establish thought leadership on LinkedIn. She starts by optimizing her profile, highlighting her extensive experience and key achievements in cybersecurity. Sarah writes detailed articles on emerging threats, shares quick tips on securing digital assets, and posts videos discussing industry news. She actively engages with her network by commenting on relevant posts and participating in cybersecurity groups.

Sarah collaborates with other cybersecurity influencers by conducting joint webinars and guest writing for industry blogs. Over time, her consistent and valuable contributions established her as a thought leader, leading to speaking invitations, consulting opportunities, and a growing follower base on LinkedIn.

Using LinkedIn for thought leadership involves a strategic approach to content creation, engagement, and collaboration. By defining your niche, optimizing your profile, creating high-quality content, engaging with your network, collaborating with influencers, and analyzing your efforts, you can build a strong thought leadership presence on LinkedIn. This presence not only enhances your credibility but also opens doors to new opportunities and strengthens your influence in your industry.

6.3 Implementing LinkedIn InMail Campaigns

LinkedIn InMail campaigns are a powerful way to connect directly with potential leads, clients, or partners through personalized messages. Unlike regular email, InMail messages can be sent to any LinkedIn member without needing a prior connection, making it a valuable tool for reaching out to prospects in a targeted and professional manner. This section will guide you through the process of implementing effective LinkedIn InMail campaigns.

Understanding LinkedIn InMail

LinkedIn InMail is a premium feature that allows users to send direct messages to LinkedIn members outside their immediate network. InMail messages have higher open and response rates compared to traditional email, largely due to the professional context and the credibility of the LinkedIn platform.

Benefits of LinkedIn InMail Campaigns

- **High Visibility**: InMail messages appear directly in the recipient's LinkedIn inbox, often accompanied by a notification, ensuring they are seen.
- **Targeted Outreach**: Advanced filtering options allow you to target specific demographics, job titles, industries, and more.
- **Personalization**: Personalized messages increase the likelihood of engagement and response.
- **Professional Context**: LinkedIn's professional environment lends credibility to your messages, making recipients more likely to take them seriously.

Steps to Implement LinkedIn InMail Campaigns

Step 1: Define Your Campaign Objectives

Before crafting your InMail messages, it's crucial to clearly define your campaign objectives. Common goals include:

- **Lead Generation**: Reaching out to potential customers or clients to generate new business leads.
- **Event Promotion**: Inviting targeted professionals to webinars, conferences, or other events.
- **Content Distribution**: Sharing valuable content such as whitepapers, case studies, or research reports to establish thought leadership.
- **Job Recruitment**: Contacting potential candidates for open positions within your organization.

Clearly defined objectives will guide the rest of your campaign strategy, from targeting to message crafting.

Step 2: Identify and Segment Your Target Audience

Use LinkedIn's advanced search and filtering options to identify and segment your target audience. Criteria for segmentation might include:

- **Job Title**: Specific roles or positions relevant to your campaign.
- **Industry**: Particular industries that align with your offerings or event.
- **Geography**: Geographic locations where your campaign will have the most impact.
- **Company Size**: Targeting companies of a certain size that would benefit from your product or service.

By narrowing down your audience, you ensure that your messages reach the most relevant recipients, increasing the chances of engagement and conversion.

Step 3: Craft Personalized InMail Messages

Personalization is key to the success of InMail campaigns. Follow these best practices when crafting your messages:

- **Subject Line**: Create a compelling and concise subject line that grabs attention and indicates the message's relevance.
- **Introduction**: Start with a personalized greeting and mention any common connections or relevant context.
- **Body**: Clearly state the purpose of your message, highlighting how it benefits the recipient. Keep the content concise and focused.
- **Call to Action (CTA)**: End with a clear and actionable CTA, whether it's scheduling a call, registering for an event, or downloading a resource.
- **Professional Tone**: Maintain a professional and respectful tone throughout your message.

Example InMail Structure:

Subject: Invitation to Exclusive Webinar on Cybersecurity Trends

Hi [Recipient's Name],

I hope this message finds you well. I noticed your expertise in [Recipient's Industry/Field], and I thought you might be interested in an upcoming webinar we are hosting on the latest trends in cybersecurity.

As a [Recipient's Job Title] at [Recipient's Company], your insights would be incredibly valuable to the discussion. The webinar will cover emerging threats and innovative defense strategies, and we'd love to have you join us.

To register, please click [Link to Registration].

Thank you for your time, and I hope to see you at the webinar.

Best regards,

[Your Name]

[Your Job Title]

[Your Company]

Step 4: Execute and Monitor Your Campaign

Once your messages are ready, it's time to execute your campaign. Use LinkedIn's Campaign Manager to send your InMails and monitor their performance. Key metrics to track include:

- **Open Rates**: The percentage of recipients who open your InMail messages.
- **Response Rates**: The percentage of recipients who respond to your messages.
- **Click-Through Rates (CTR)**: The percentage of recipients who click on links within your InMail.
- **Conversion Rates**: The percentage of recipients who complete the desired action, such as registering for an event or scheduling a call.

Step 5: Analyze and Optimize

After your campaign has run for a sufficient period, analyze the results to determine its effectiveness. Identify which aspects of your campaign performed well and which areas need improvement. Use these insights to optimize future InMail campaigns.

Consider A/B testing different subject lines, message content, or CTAs to see what resonates best with your audience. Continuously refining your approach will lead to better results over time.

Implementing LinkedIn InMail campaigns can significantly enhance your ability to connect with potential leads, promote events, distribute content, and recruit top talent. By defining clear objectives, targeting the right audience, crafting personalized messages, and analyzing performance, you can create effective InMail campaigns that drive meaningful engagement and achieve your business goals. In the next section, we will explore additional advanced LinkedIn marketing tactics to further boost your success on the platform.

6.4 LinkedIn Events and Webinars

LinkedIn Events and Webinars are potent tools for engaging with your audience, showcasing your expertise, and generating leads. These features allow you to create virtual or in-person events, invite your network, and promote your content to a broader audience. This section will guide you through planning, promoting, and hosting successful LinkedIn Events and Webinars.

Understanding LinkedIn Events and Webinars

LinkedIn Events is a feature that lets you create and manage professional events directly on the platform. It provides a streamlined way to promote your event, invite attendees, and engage with your audience before, during, and after the event. Webinars, often hosted via LinkedIn Live, allow you to broadcast live video content to your audience, facilitating real-time interaction and engagement.

Benefits of LinkedIn Events and Webinars

- **Wide Reach**: Leverage your LinkedIn network to reach a large, professional audience.
- **Engagement**: Foster real-time interaction and engagement with your audience.
- **Lead Generation**: Capture leads and build relationships with potential customers.
- **Brand Authority**: Establish your brand as a thought leader in your industry.

Steps to Implement LinkedIn Events and Webinars

Step 1: Plan Your Event or Webinar

Effective planning is crucial for a successful LinkedIn Event or Webinar. Start by defining the purpose and objectives of your event. Common goals include:

- **Educational Content**: Share valuable insights, tips, or industry knowledge.
- **Product Launch**: Introduce a new product or service to your audience.
- **Networking**: Facilitate connections among industry professionals.
- **Lead Generation**: Capture contact information and engage potential customers.

Determine the format of your event, whether it's a panel discussion, a solo presentation, a Q&A session, or a combination of these. Also, set a date and time that will be convenient for your target audience.

Step 2: Create Your LinkedIn Event

To create a LinkedIn Event:

- **Navigate to LinkedIn Events**: On your LinkedIn homepage, click the "Work" icon and select "Events."
- **Create Event**: Click the "Create" button and fill in the details of your event, including the event name, date, time, description, and cover image. Ensure your description is clear and compelling, outlining the key benefits of attending.
- **Event Settings**: Choose whether your event is public or private. Public events are visible to anyone on LinkedIn, while private events are only accessible to guests.
- **Add Speakers and Hosts**: Include the names and profiles of any speakers or hosts to build credibility and attract attendees.

Step 3: Promote Your Event

Promotion is key to attracting attendees to your event or webinar. Use the following strategies to maximize reach:

- **Invite Connections**: Personally invite your LinkedIn connections who might be interested in your event.
- **Share on LinkedIn**: Post about your event on your LinkedIn feed and in relevant LinkedIn Groups. Use engaging visuals and highlight the benefits of attending.
- **Sponsored Content**: Consider using LinkedIn Sponsored Content to promote your event to a broader audience.
- **Email Marketing**: Send invitations and reminders to your email list, including a link to the LinkedIn Event page.
- **Cross-Promotion**: Promote your event on other social media platforms and your website.

Step 4: Host Your Event or Webinar

On the day of the event, ensure everything is set up and ready to go:

- **Technical Setup**: Test your audio, video, and internet connection beforehand to avoid technical issues.
- **Engage Your Audience**: Encourage participation through Q&A sessions, polls, and interactive discussions.
- **Deliver Value**: Focus on providing valuable content that meets the needs and interests of your audience.

- **Moderate Effectively**: Assign a moderator to manage the event, handle technical issues, and facilitate audience interaction.

Step 5: Follow Up and Analyze

After the event, follow up with attendees to keep the engagement going:

- **Thank You Messages**: Send personalized thank-you messages to attendees, along with any promised resources or recordings of the event.
- **Feedback**: Ask for feedback to understand what worked well and what could be improved.
- **Nurture Leads**: Add attendees to your CRM and nurture them with relevant content and offers.

Analyze the performance of your event to measure its success:

- **Attendance Rate**: Compare the number of attendees to the number of registrations.
- **Engagement Metrics**: Track engagement during the event, such as questions asked, poll responses, and chat activity.
- **Post-Event Actions**: Monitor actions taken by attendees after the event, such as visiting your website, downloading resources, or contacting your sales team.

Example Scenario

Imagine a marketing consultancy firm, BrightMinds, planning to host a webinar on "The Future of Digital Marketing." They start by defining their goal: educating their audience on emerging trends. They create a LinkedIn Event, detailing the date, time, and a compelling description.

To promote the webinar, BrightMinds invites their LinkedIn connections, shares the event on their company page, and uses LinkedIn Sponsored Content to reach a wider audience. They also send email invitations to their subscribers.

On the day of the webinar, BrightMinds ensures their technical setup is flawless and engages the audience through interactive polls and a Q&A session. After the event, they follow up with attendees, thanking them and sharing the webinar recording. They also analyze the engagement metrics and feedback to refine their future webinars.

LinkedIn Events and Webinars offer a dynamic way to engage with your audience, showcase your expertise, and generate leads. By carefully planning, promoting, and hosting your event, and following up with attendees, you can create impactful experiences that drive meaningful engagement and business growth. In the next section, we will explore additional advanced LinkedIn marketing tactics to further enhance your strategy.

6.5 Collaborations and Influencer Marketing

Collaborations and influencer marketing on LinkedIn are powerful strategies to amplify your reach, enhance brand credibility, and engage with a broader audience. By partnering with industry influencers and collaborating with other professionals or brands, you can leverage their established networks and reputations to achieve your marketing goals. This section will delve into the strategies and best practices for successful collaborations and influencer marketing on LinkedIn.

Understanding Collaborations and Influencer Marketing

Collaborations involve working with other professionals or brands to create and promote content, events, or campaigns. These partnerships can lead to shared resources, audiences, and expertise, resulting in mutually beneficial outcomes.

Influencer marketing involves partnering with individuals who have a significant following and influence within your industry. These influencers can help promote your products, services, or content to their audience, lending their credibility and reach to your brand.

Benefits of Collaboration and Influencer Marketing

- **Extended Reach**: Access new and larger audiences through the influencer's or collaborator's network.
- **Enhanced Credibility**: Gain trust and credibility by associating with respected industry figures.
- **Increased Engagement**: Boost engagement through authentic and relatable content created by influencers or collaborators.
- **Content Diversity**: Introduce fresh perspectives and ideas to your content strategy.

Steps to Implement Collaborations and Influencer Marketing

Step 1: Identify Potential Collaborators and Influencers

Begin by identifying professionals, brands, or influencers who align with your industry, values, and target audience. Consider the following:

- **Relevance**: Ensure the collaborator or influencer has expertise and influence in areas related to your business.
- **Reach**: Look for individuals or brands with a substantial and engaged following.
- **Reputation**: Partner with those who have a positive reputation and align with your brand values.
- **Engagement**: Focus on influencers with high engagement rates, as this indicates an active and interested audience.

Step 2: Establish Clear Objectives and Goals

Define the objectives and goals for your collaboration or influencer campaign. Common goals include:

- **Brand Awareness**: Increase visibility and recognition of your brand.
- **Lead Generation**: Attract potential customers and capture leads.
- **Content Creation**: Produce high-quality, diverse content that resonates with your audience.
- **Event Promotion**: Promote events, webinars, or product launches.

Having clear objectives will guide your strategy and ensure all parties are aligned on the desired outcomes.

Step 3: Develop a Mutually Beneficial Proposal

When reaching out to potential collaborators or influencers, develop a proposal that highlights the mutual benefits of the partnership. Your proposal should include:

- **Purpose**: Clearly state the purpose and goals of the collaboration.
- **Benefits**: Explain how the partnership will benefit both parties, such as increased exposure, shared content, or new audience engagement.
- **Scope**: Define the scope of the collaboration, including content types, frequency, and responsibilities.
- **Compensation**: If applicable, outline any compensation, incentives, or other forms of value exchange.

Step 4: Create Engaging Collaborative Content

Collaborate with your partner to create content that leverages both parties' strengths and resonates with your combined audience. Types of collaborative content include:

- **Guest Posts and Articles**: Write guest posts for each other's LinkedIn profiles or blogs, sharing expertise and insights.

- **Webinars and Live Sessions**: Co-host webinars or live sessions on LinkedIn, discussing industry trends, providing educational content, or conducting interviews.
- **Joint Campaigns**: Develop joint marketing campaigns that include shared posts, videos, or graphics.
- **Interviews and Features**: Feature each other in interviews, podcasts, or case studies, highlighting collaborative achievements and insights.

Step 5: Promote and Amplify the Collaboration

Promote the collaborative content through both parties' LinkedIn profiles, company pages, and other social media platforms. Strategies for promotion include:

- **Cross-Promotion**: Share each other's content to maximize reach and engagement.
- **Sponsored Content**: Use LinkedIn Sponsored Content to extend the reach of your collaborative posts.
- **Engagement**: Encourage both audiences to engage with the content through comments, likes, and shares.
- **Hashtags**: Use relevant hashtags to increase visibility and attract a broader audience.

Step 6: Measure and Analyze Results

Track and analyze the performance of your collaboration or influencer campaign to assess its effectiveness. Key metrics to monitor include:

- **Engagement Rates**: Measure likes, comments, shares, and overall interaction with the content.
- **Reach and Impressions**: Track the total reach and impressions to gauge visibility.
- **Lead Generation**: Monitor the number of leads or conversions generated from the campaign.
- **Feedback**: Collect feedback from your audience and your partner to understand what worked well and what could be improved.

Example Scenario

Imagine a fitness technology company, FitTech, aiming to promote their new wearable device. They identify a popular fitness influencer, Jane, with a large and engaged following on LinkedIn. FitTech reaches out to Jane with a proposal to collaborate on a series of posts and a live webinar discussing the benefits of the new device.

Jane agrees, and together they create engaging content, including guest articles, product reviews, and a live Q&A session. FitTech promotes the collaboration through its LinkedIn company page and sponsors some of Jane's posts to extend its reach.

The collaboration results in increased brand awareness, high engagement rates, and a significant number of leads for FitTech. Jane also benefits from the partnership by offering valuable content to her audience and gaining credibility through the association with a reputable brand.

Collaborations and influencer marketing on LinkedIn can significantly enhance your marketing efforts by expanding your reach, building credibility, and increasing engagement. By carefully identifying potential partners, establishing clear goals, creating engaging content, and analyzing the results, you can create successful partnerships that drive meaningful business outcomes. In the next section, we will explore more advanced LinkedIn marketing tactics to further optimize your strategy.

Chapter 7: Engaging and Converting Your Audience

Engaging and converting your audience on LinkedIn is essential for achieving your marketing objectives, whether it's generating leads, increasing brand awareness, or driving sales. This chapter explores effective strategies to captivate your audience's attention, foster meaningful interactions, and ultimately convert them into loyal customers or clients.

Understanding Audience Engagement

Audience engagement on LinkedIn goes beyond likes and shares; it involves creating valuable interactions that resonate with your audience and encourage them to take action. Engaged audiences are more likely to consume your content, interact with your brand, and advocate for your products or services.

Strategies to Enhance Audience Engagement and Conversions

1. Create Compelling Content

Content is king on LinkedIn. To capture and maintain your audience's interest, focus on:

- **Relevant Topics**: Address industry trends, challenges, and solutions that matter to your audience.

- **Visual Appeal**: Use eye-catching visuals, such as infographics, videos, and images, to enhance your content's appeal.
- **Educational Value**: Provide insights, tips, and actionable advice that add value to your audience's professional lives.
- **Consistency**: Maintain a regular posting schedule to stay top of mind and build credibility.

2. Foster Meaningful Interactions

Encourage conversations and interactions with your audience through:

- **Engaging Posts**: Pose questions, encourage comments, and invite opinions to spark discussions.
- **Respond Promptly**: Acknowledge and respond to comments and messages promptly to show genuine interest and build rapport.
- **LinkedIn Polls**: Use polls to gather insights, opinions, and feedback from your audience.
- **Live Video**: Host live Q&A sessions, webinars, or product demonstrations to interact with your audience in real-time.

3. Personalize Your Approach

Tailor your content and messaging to resonate with different segments of your audience:

- **Segmentation**: Use LinkedIn's targeting options to segment your audience based on job title, industry, location, etc., and personalize your messaging accordingly.
- **Personalized Messaging**: Address your audience by name, acknowledge their interests or pain points, and offer personalized solutions or recommendations.

4. Utilize LinkedIn Features Effectively

Take advantage of LinkedIn features to enhance engagement and conversions:

- **LinkedIn Articles**: Publish long-form articles to dive deep into topics, showcase thought leadership, and provide in-depth insights.
- **LinkedIn Groups**: Participate in and create LinkedIn Groups to foster community engagement, share expertise, and build relationships.
- **LinkedIn Ads**: Use targeted LinkedIn ads to reach specific audience segments and drive traffic to your content or landing pages.

5. Measure and Optimize Performance

Regularly monitor key metrics to gauge the effectiveness of your engagement strategies:

- **Engagement Metrics**: Track likes, comments, shares, and click-through rates (CTR) to assess content performance.
- **Conversion Metrics**: Measure conversions, such as form submissions, downloads, or purchases attributed to LinkedIn activities.
- **A/B Testing**: Experiment with different content formats, messaging styles, and posting times to identify what resonates best with your audience.

Example Scenario

Consider a software-as-a-service (SaaS) company, CloudSolutions, aiming to engage and convert IT professionals on LinkedIn. They create a content strategy that includes regular posts addressing cloud computing trends, cybersecurity challenges, and software development best practices. CloudSolutions hosts live webinars featuring industry experts, where attendees can ask questions and learn about the company's solutions.

CloudSolutions actively participates in relevant LinkedIn Groups, offering valuable advice and building relationships with group members. They use LinkedIn Ads to promote their webinars and whitepapers, targeting IT managers and decision-makers.

Through consistent engagement, personalized interactions, and valuable content, CloudSolutions establishes itself as a trusted authority in the industry, driving increased website traffic, lead generation, and conversions from LinkedIn.

Engaging and converting your audience on LinkedIn requires a strategic approach centered around creating compelling content, fostering meaningful interactions, personalizing your messaging, leveraging

LinkedIn features, and continuously optimizing your strategies based on performance data. By implementing these strategies effectively, you can build a loyal and engaged LinkedIn community that supports your business goals and drives sustainable growth. In the following sections, we will explore advanced LinkedIn marketing tactics to further enhance your audience engagement and conversion efforts.

7.1 Best Practices for Engagement

Effective engagement on LinkedIn is crucial for building relationships, establishing thought leadership, and driving business outcomes. This section outlines key best practices to maximize engagement with your audience on the platform.

1. Know Your Audience

Understanding your audience is foundational to creating relevant and compelling content. Use LinkedIn's analytics and insights to gather information about your followers:

- **Demographics**: Know their job titles, industries, locations, and seniority levels.
- **Interests**: Identify topics and trends that resonate with your audience.
- **Behavior**: Track engagement metrics to understand what types of content they prefer and when they are most active.

2. Create Valuable Content

Content that provides value to your audience is more likely to generate engagement. Consider these strategies:

- **Educational Content**: Share industry insights, tips, and best practices that help solve your audience's challenges.
- **Visual Content**: Use images, videos, and infographics to make your content visually appealing and easier to consume.
- **Storytelling**: Share stories, case studies, and personal experiences that resonate with your audience emotionally.

3. Encourage Conversation

Engage your audience in meaningful conversations to foster community and interaction:

- **Ask Questions**: Pose thought-provoking questions to encourage comments and discussions.
- **Respond Promptly**: Acknowledge and respond to comments promptly to demonstrate engagement and build relationships.
- **LinkedIn Polls**: Use polls to gather opinions, preferences, and feedback from your audience.

4. Utilize LinkedIn Features

Take advantage of LinkedIn's features to enhance engagement:

- **LinkedIn Articles**: Publish long-form content to dive deep into topics and showcase thought leadership.
- **LinkedIn Live**: Host live video sessions, webinars, or Q&A sessions to interact with your audience in real time.
- **LinkedIn Groups**: Join and participate in relevant groups to share expertise, network with peers, and engage in discussions.

5. Personalize Your Interactions

Tailor your messaging to resonate with individual members of your audience:

- **Segmentation**: Use LinkedIn's targeting options to segment your audience based on their interests, job roles, or industries.
- **Personalized Messaging**: Address your audience by name and tailor your content to address their specific needs or pain points.

6. Be Consistent and Authentic

Consistency and authenticity are key to building trust and maintaining engagement:

- **Posting Schedule**: Maintain a regular posting schedule to stay top-of-mind with your audience.

- **Authenticity**: Be genuine in your interactions and content, showing your personality and values as a brand.

7. Measure and Optimize

Monitor your engagement metrics to evaluate the effectiveness of your efforts:

- **Engagement Metrics**: Track likes, comments, shares, and click-through rates (CTR) to gauge content performance.
- **Conversion Metrics**: Measure conversions such as form submissions, downloads, or sign-ups attributed to LinkedIn activities.
- **A/B Testing**: Experiment with different content formats, messaging styles, and posting times to identify what resonates best with your audience.

Example Scenario

Imagine a digital marketing agency, MarketTrends, targeting small businesses on LinkedIn. They research to understand their audience's challenges and interests in digital marketing. Based on their findings, MarketTrends creates a content calendar that includes informative blog posts, how-to videos, and client success stories.

To encourage engagement, MarketTrends asks their audience questions in their posts, responds to comments promptly, and hosts monthly LinkedIn Live sessions where they discuss digital marketing trends and answer questions from viewers. They also join relevant LinkedIn Groups to share their expertise and build relationships with group members.

By consistently providing valuable content, fostering conversations, and leveraging LinkedIn features effectively, MarketTrends increases engagement with its audience, strengthens its brand presence, and generates leads for its services.

Implementing these best practices for engagement on LinkedIn can help you build a strong presence, foster meaningful connections, and achieve your marketing goals. By understanding your audience, creating valuable content, encouraging conversations, utilizing LinkedIn features, personalizing interactions, and measuring your results, you can effectively engage with your audience and drive business success on the platform. In the following sections, we will explore advanced LinkedIn marketing tactics to further enhance your engagement strategies.

7.2 Personalizing Your Interactions

Personalizing your interactions on LinkedIn is essential for building meaningful relationships, increasing engagement, and driving conversions. This section explores effective strategies for tailoring your messaging and content to resonate with individual members of your audience.

Why Personalization Matters

Personalization demonstrates that you understand your audience's needs, interests, and preferences, which can significantly enhance the effectiveness of your communication efforts on LinkedIn. It helps create a more relevant and engaging experience for your connections, fostering stronger connections and driving deeper engagement.

Strategies for Personalizing Your Interactions

1. Audience Segmentation

Segment your audience based on relevant criteria such as:

- **Job Title and Function**: Tailor your messaging based on the roles and responsibilities of your connections.
- **Industry**: Customize your content to address industry-specific challenges and trends.
- **Location**: Consider regional differences that may impact your audience's needs and preferences.
- **Engagement Level**: Adjust your approach based on how actively your connections interact with your content.

By segmenting your audience, you can create more targeted and personalized messaging that resonates with specific groups within your network.

2. Address Connections by Name

Addressing your connections by name adds a personal touch to your interactions and demonstrates that your message is intended specifically for them. Use LinkedIn's personalization features to address your audience members by their first names in messages and comments.

3. Tailor Content to Pain Points and Interests

Create content that addresses the pain points, challenges, and interests of your audience:

- **Educational Content**: Provide insights, tips, and solutions that directly address the issues your connections face in their professional roles.
- **Relevant Examples**: Share case studies, success stories, or examples that resonate with your audience's specific needs and goals.
- **Industry Insights**: Offer perspectives on industry trends and developments that are relevant to your connections' interests.

4. Customize Messaging Based on Engagement History

Tailor your messaging based on your audience's past interactions with your content:

- **Follow-Up Messages**: Send personalized follow-up messages to connections who have engaged with your posts, articles, or comments.

- **Recommendations**: Offer personalized recommendations for content, resources, or solutions based on their previous engagements.

5. Use LinkedIn's Targeting Options

Take advantage of LinkedIn's targeting options to deliver personalized content and messages:

- **Company Size and Type**: Customize your messaging based on the size and type of organizations your connections work for.
- **Seniority Level**: Adjust your approach depending on whether you are engaging with executives, mid-level managers, or entry-level professionals.
- **Interest Targeting**: Target specific interests or skills listed on profiles to tailor your content accordingly.

6. Engage Proactively and Responsively

Initiate conversations and respond promptly to comments and messages from your connections:

- **Proactive Engagement**: Reach out to connections with personalized messages, invitations to events, or requests for feedback.

- **Timely Responses**: Demonstrate responsiveness by promptly replying to comments, questions, and inquiries from your audience.

Example Scenario

Imagine a financial advisory firm, WealthWell Advisors, specializing in retirement planning. They personalize their interactions on LinkedIn by segmenting their audience into categories such as young professionals, mid-career executives, and retirees. WealthWell Advisors create tailored content for each segment, addressing their unique financial goals and concerns.

For instance, they publish articles on retirement savings strategies for young professionals, investment opportunities for mid-career executives, and estate planning tips for retirees. They also use LinkedIn's messaging feature to send personalized invitations to webinars and seminars based on their audience's interests and engagement history.

By personalizing their interactions, WealthWell Advisors build trust, establish themselves as experts in retirement planning, and attract a loyal following of clients and prospects seeking personalized financial advice.

Personalizing your interactions on LinkedIn is a powerful strategy for enhancing engagement, building relationships, and driving conversions. By segmenting your audience, addressing connections by name, tailoring content to their pain points and interests, customizing messaging based on engagement history, leveraging LinkedIn's targeting options, and engaging proactively and responsively, you can create a more personalized and impactful experience for your audience. In the following sections, we will explore advanced LinkedIn marketing tactics to further optimize your personalized interaction strategies.

7.3 Building Trust and Authority

Building trust and authority on LinkedIn is crucial for establishing credibility, attracting a loyal audience, and driving business growth. This section explores effective strategies to cultivate trust and position yourself as a trusted authority within your industry on the platform.

Why Trust and Authority Matter

Trust is the foundation of any successful professional relationship. Establishing authority demonstrates your expertise and leadership in your field, making it more likely for your audience to value your insights, engage with your content, and ultimately choose your products or services.

Strategies for Building Trust and Authority on LinkedIn

1. Provide Valuable and High-Quality Content

Deliver content that educates, informs, and adds value to your audience's professional lives:

- **Thought Leadership**: Share original insights, opinions, and perspectives on industry trends and developments.
- **Educational Resources**: Offer practical tips, guides, and resources that address your audience's challenges and needs.

- **Case Studies and Success Stories**: Showcase real-life examples and results to illustrate your expertise and credibility.

2. Be Authentic and Transparent

Authenticity builds trust by demonstrating sincerity and integrity in your interactions:

- **Personal Branding**: Share your personal experiences, journey, and professional achievements to humanize your brand.
- **Open Communication**: Be transparent about your offerings, policies, and practices to build credibility with your audience.

3. Engage Consistently and Responsively

Regularly engage with your audience through meaningful interactions:

- **Timely Responses**: Respond promptly to comments, messages, and inquiries to demonstrate attentiveness and respect.
- **Proactive Engagement**: Initiate conversations, ask questions, and seek feedback from your audience to foster engagement.

4. Showcase Social Proof and Endorsements

Highlight testimonials, client success stories, and endorsements from satisfied customers or industry peers:

- **Recommendations**: Request and showcase LinkedIn recommendations from clients, colleagues, or partners to validate your expertise.
- **Case Studies**: Share detailed case studies that demonstrate the positive impact of your products or services on clients' businesses.

5. Participate in Industry Conversations

Engage in discussions and share insights within LinkedIn Groups, posts, and comments:

- **Thoughtful Contributions**: Provide valuable contributions to discussions by sharing expertise, insights, and best practices.
- **Networking**: Connect with industry influencers, thought leaders and peers to expand your network and visibility.

6. Leverage LinkedIn's Publishing Platform

Publish long-form articles on LinkedIn to establish thought leadership and showcase your expertise:

- **Original Content**: Create in-depth articles that delve into complex topics, offer solutions, or present industry insights.
- **SEO Optimization**: Use relevant keywords and tags to increase the discoverability of your articles within LinkedIn and search engines.

7. Demonstrate Consistent Professionalism

Maintain a professional and polished presence on LinkedIn:

- **Profile Optimization**: Ensure your LinkedIn profile is complete, up-to-date, and reflects your expertise and achievements.
- **Brand Voice**: Maintain a consistent brand voice and messaging across your LinkedIn activities to reinforce your professional identity.

Example Scenario

Imagine a digital marketing consultant, Sarah, specializing in SEO strategies. Sarah builds trust and authority on LinkedIn by regularly sharing case studies of successful SEO campaigns, offering practical tips for improving search engine rankings and participating in discussions within relevant LinkedIn Groups.

Sarah also publishes weekly LinkedIn articles that explore advanced SEO techniques and best practices. By consistently providing valuable insights, engaging with her audience, and showcasing her expertise, Sarah establishes herself as a trusted authority in the field of digital marketing.

Building trust and authority on LinkedIn requires a strategic approach focused on delivering valuable content, demonstrating authenticity, engaging consistently, showcasing social proof, participating in industry conversations, leveraging LinkedIn's publishing platform, and maintaining professionalism. By implementing these strategies effectively, you can enhance your credibility, attract a loyal following, and position yourself as a respected leader within your industry on LinkedIn. In the following sections, we will explore advanced LinkedIn marketing tactics to further strengthen your trust and authority-building efforts.

7.4 Turning Connections into Leads

Converting LinkedIn connections into leads is a critical objective for businesses looking to leverage the platform for lead generation. This section explores effective strategies to nurture your LinkedIn connections and turn them into valuable leads for your business.

Understanding the Lead Generation Process on LinkedIn

LinkedIn offers a robust platform for connecting with professionals, building relationships, and ultimately converting those connections into leads. The process involves:

- **Connecting**: Establish connections with relevant professionals, prospects, and decision-makers within your target audience.
- **Engaging**: Build rapport and trust through meaningful interactions, content sharing, and engagement activities.
- **Converting**: Encourage connections to take action, such as signing up for webinars, downloading resources, or requesting consultations.

Strategies for Turning Connections into Leads

1. Define Your Target Audience

Identify and target professionals who are likely to be interested in your products or services:

- **Ideal Customer Profile**: Develop detailed personas based on job titles, industries, company sizes, and other relevant criteria.
- **LinkedIn Search and Filters**: Use LinkedIn's search and filtering options to find and connect with your target audience.

2. Provide Value through Content

Offer valuable and relevant content that addresses your audience's pain points and interests:

- **Educational Resources**: Share whitepapers, e-books, guides, and case studies that showcase your expertise and provide solutions.
- **Webinars and Workshops**: Host informative webinars or workshops on topics of interest to your connections.

3. Engage Actively and Consistently

Build relationships through consistent engagement and personalized interactions:

- Comment and Like Engage with your connections' posts by commenting thoughtfully and liking their updates.
- LinkedIn Messaging: Send personalized messages to share resources, invite connections to events, or offer consultations.

4. Use LinkedIn Lead Generation Forms

Utilize LinkedIn's Lead Gen Forms to capture leads directly from your ads or sponsored content:

- **Customizable Forms**: Create forms with fields that capture relevant information from prospects, such as name, email, job title, and company.
- **Automated Lead Collection**: Automatically collect leads directly into your LinkedIn Campaign Manager or integrate with your CRM system.

5. Leverage LinkedIn Groups

Participate in and create LinkedIn Groups relevant to your industry or target audience:

- **Thought Leadership**: Share valuable insights, participate in discussions, and establish yourself as an industry authority.
- **Lead Generation Posts**: Occasionally share lead-generating content, such as webinars or e-books, within LinkedIn Groups.

6. Nurture Leads through LinkedIn Messaging

Use LinkedIn Messaging to nurture leads and move them through the sales funnel:

- **Personalized Follow-Ups**: Send personalized follow-up messages to leads who have engaged with your content or shown interest in your offerings.
- **Provide Solutions**: Offer tailored solutions or recommendations based on the prospect's needs and challenges.

7. Measure and Optimize Lead Generation Efforts

Monitor key metrics to assess the effectiveness of your lead generation strategies:

- **Conversion Rates**: Track the number of leads generated from LinkedIn activities and campaigns.
- **Engagement Metrics**: Analyze likes, comments, shares, and click-through rates to gauge audience interest and interaction.
- **A/B Testing**: Experiment with different messaging, content formats, and calls-to-action (CTAs) to optimize lead generation performance.

Example Scenario

Consider a software company, TechSolutions, specializing in cybersecurity solutions. TechSolutions targets IT professionals and decision-makers on LinkedIn by sharing informative content about cybersecurity threats, best practices, and case studies demonstrating their solutions' effectiveness.

They utilize LinkedIn Lead Gen Forms in sponsored content campaigns to capture leads interested in their cybersecurity webinars. TechSolutions follows up with leads through personalized LinkedIn messages, offering free consultations and tailored solutions based on the prospects' cybersecurity needs.

By consistently providing value, engaging actively, and leveraging LinkedIn's lead generation tools, TechSolutions successfully converts LinkedIn connections into qualified leads, driving business growth and expanding its customer base.

Turning LinkedIn connections into leads requires a strategic approach focused on providing value through content, engaging actively with your audience, leveraging LinkedIn's lead generation tools, nurturing leads through personalized interactions, and continuously optimizing your lead generation efforts based on performance data. By implementing these strategies effectively, you can maximize your lead generation potential on LinkedIn and achieve your business objectives. In the following sections, we will explore advanced LinkedIn marketing tactics to further enhance your lead generation strategies.

7.5 Case Studies of Successful Engagement and Conversion

Examining case studies of successful engagement and conversion on LinkedIn provides valuable insights into effective strategies and tactics employed by businesses to achieve their marketing goals. This section explores notable examples where companies have effectively engaged their audience and converted LinkedIn interactions into tangible business outcomes.

Case Study 1: Company XYZ's Thought Leadership Campaign

Objective: Company XYZ, a management consulting firm, aimed to establish thought leadership in the healthcare industry.

Strategy:

- **Content Strategy**: Company XYZ developed a comprehensive content strategy focused on addressing healthcare industry challenges, trends, and best practices.
- **LinkedIn Articles**: They published regular LinkedIn articles written by their industry experts, offering insights and thought-provoking analyses.
- **Engagement Tactics**: They actively engaged with their audience by responding to comments, participating in LinkedIn Groups, and sharing valuable resources.

Results:

- **Increased Visibility**: Company XYZ's thought leadership articles gained significant traction, increasing its visibility within the healthcare community.

- **Engagement Metrics**: They saw a notable increase in likes, comments, and shares on their LinkedIn content, indicating strong audience engagement.
- **Lead Generation**: The thought leadership campaign generated qualified leads interested in consulting services, resulting in new client acquisitions.

Case Study 2: TechSolutions' Webinar Series

Objective: TechSolutions, a cybersecurity company, aimed to generate leads and educate IT professionals on cybersecurity best practices.

Strategy:

- **Webinar Series**: TechSolutions hosted a series of webinars on LinkedIn addressing various cybersecurity topics, such as data protection and threat prevention.
- **Promotion**: They promoted their webinars using LinkedIn ads and sponsored content, targeting IT decision-makers and security professionals.
- **LinkedIn Groups**: They shared webinar announcements and engaged in discussions within relevant LinkedIn Groups focused on cybersecurity.

Results:

- **High Attendance Rates**: The webinar series attracted a large number of attendees interested in learning about cybersecurity solutions.
- **Lead Generation**: Through LinkedIn Lead Gen Forms integrated with their webinar registrations, TechSolutions captured valuable leads interested in their cybersecurity services.
- **ROI**: The campaign resulted in a significant return on investment (ROI), with a notable increase in sales opportunities and new client contracts.

Case Study 3: Marketing Agency's Content Marketing Campaign

Objective: A digital marketing agency aimed to showcase its expertise and attract new clients through content marketing on LinkedIn.

Strategy:

- **Content Diversity**: They diversified their content strategy to include blog posts, infographics, and client success stories showcasing their marketing results.
- **LinkedIn Pulse**: Leveraging LinkedIn Pulse, they published engaging articles on digital marketing trends and strategies, positioning themselves as industry leaders.
- **Engagement and Outreach**: They actively engaged with LinkedIn connections through personalized messages, offering free consultations and audits.

Results:

- **Brand Authority**: The agency established a strong reputation as an expert in digital marketing, gaining recognition from industry peers and potential clients.
- **Lead Generation**: Their content marketing efforts generated a steady flow of qualified leads interested in digital marketing services.
- **Client Acquisition**: They successfully converted LinkedIn connections into long-term clients, resulting in increased revenue and business growth.

Key Takeaways

These case studies illustrate successful engagement and conversion strategies on LinkedIn:

- **Content Strategy**: Develop valuable and relevant content tailored to your audience's interests and needs.
- **Active Engagement**: Actively participating in discussions, responding to comments, and leveraging LinkedIn Groups.
- **Targeted Promotion**: Using LinkedIn ads and sponsored content to reach and engage specific target audiences.
- **Lead Generation Tactics**: Integrating LinkedIn Lead Gen Forms and personalized outreach to nurture leads effectively.

By learning from these successful examples and adapting proven strategies to your own LinkedIn marketing efforts, you can enhance engagement, drive conversions, and achieve your business objectives effectively on the platform.

Case studies of successful engagement and conversion on LinkedIn highlight the importance of strategic planning, compelling content creation, active engagement with your audience, and effective use of LinkedIn's features for lead generation and business growth. By implementing these strategies thoughtfully and consistently, businesses can capitalize on LinkedIn's potential as a powerful platform for building relationships, establishing authority, and driving meaningful business outcomes. In the following sections, we will explore advanced LinkedIn marketing tactics to further optimize your engagement and conversion strategies.

Chapter 8: Future Trends and Innovations in LinkedIn Marketing

As LinkedIn continues to evolve as a dynamic platform for professional networking and marketing, staying ahead of emerging trends and innovations is crucial for maximizing its potential. This chapter explores future trends and innovations shaping the landscape of LinkedIn marketing.

1. Rise of Video Content

Video content is poised to play a pivotal role in LinkedIn marketing strategies:

- **Live Video**: Increasing popularity of live streaming for real-time engagement with audiences.
- **Native Video**: Enhanced visibility and engagement through LinkedIn's native video feature.
- **Personalized Video Messages**: Use of personalized video messages for direct and impactful communication.

2. AI and Automation Integration

Artificial Intelligence (AI) and automation technologies are transforming LinkedIn marketing:

- **Chatbots**: Use of AI-powered chatbots for instant responses and lead qualification.
- **Predictive Analytics**: Leveraging AI for predictive insights into audience behavior and content performance.
- **Automated Campaign Management**: Streamlining ad management and content distribution processes.

3. Personalization at Scale

Advanced personalization techniques will drive deeper connections with LinkedIn audiences:

- **Dynamic Content**: Tailoring content based on user data and behavior.
- **Hyper-targeted Campaigns**: Precision targeting using advanced segmentation and AI algorithms.
- **Account-Based Marketing (ABM)**: Personalizing outreach and content for specific companies and decision-makers.

4. Enhanced Analytics and Measurement

LinkedIn's analytics capabilities will evolve to provide deeper insights and measurement tools:

- **Attribution Modeling**: Understanding the impact of various touchpoints on conversion paths.

- **Cross-Platform Insights**: Integrating LinkedIn data with other marketing channels for holistic analysis.
- **Real-Time Reporting**: Instant access to campaign performance metrics for agile optimization.

5. Augmented Reality (AR) and Virtual Reality (VR)

Integration of AR and VR technologies for immersive brand experiences and engagement:

- **Virtual Events**: Hosting virtual conferences, product demos, and networking events.
- **AR Advertising**: Interactive ads and product demonstrations using augmented reality.
- **Virtual Tours**: Showcasing products, services, or company culture through virtual tours.

6. Sustainability and Corporate Social Responsibility (CSR)

The growing importance of sustainability and CSR initiatives in LinkedIn marketing:

- **Brand Values Alignment**: Communicating corporate values and sustainability efforts.
- **Cause-Related Campaigns**: Engaging audiences through purpose-driven marketing initiatives.

- **Employee Advocacy**: Empowering employees to promote CSR initiatives and company values.

7. Privacy and Data Security

Emphasis on privacy compliance and data security in LinkedIn marketing practices:

- **GDPR and CCPA Compliance**: Adhering to global data protection regulations.
- **Transparency**: Providing clear information on data usage and privacy policies.
- **Data Protection Measures**: Implementing robust security measures to safeguard user information.

The future of LinkedIn marketing is shaped by innovation, technological advancements, and evolving user expectations. By embracing emerging trends such as video content, AI and automation, personalized marketing, enhanced analytics, AR/VR experiences, sustainability initiatives, and prioritizing data privacy, businesses can stay ahead in leveraging LinkedIn's potential for effective communication, engagement, and lead generation. Adapting to these trends will not only enhance brand visibility and reputation but also drive meaningful connections and business growth on the world's largest professional networking platform.

In the following sections, we will delve deeper into practical strategies and implementation guidelines to capitalize on these future trends in LinkedIn marketing.

8.1 The Evolving LinkedIn Landscape

The LinkedIn landscape is continuously evolving, shaped by technological advancements, user behavior changes, and shifting market dynamics. Understanding these transformations is essential for marketers to stay ahead and effectively leverage LinkedIn for business growth. This section explores key aspects of the evolving LinkedIn landscape.

Enhanced User Experience and Interface

LinkedIn is constantly updating its user interface and features to enhance user experience:

- **Intuitive Navigation**: Simplified navigation with a cleaner layout and more accessible features.
- **Mobile Optimization**: Improved mobile app functionality, making it easier for users to engage on the go.
- **Personalized Feeds**: Algorithms that deliver more relevant content to users based on their interests and interactions.

Expansion of Content Formats

The variety of content formats available on LinkedIn has expanded, offering more ways to engage audiences:

- **LinkedIn Stories**: Short, engaging video content that disappears after 24 hours, similar to Instagram and Facebook Stories.
- **Document Sharing**: Ability to upload and share documents such as PDFs, presentations, and whitepapers directly in posts.
- **Polls**: Interactive polls that allow users to engage with content and provide feedback.

Growth of Video and Live Streaming

Video content and live streaming are becoming increasingly popular on LinkedIn:

- **Native Video Uploads**: Users can upload and share video content directly on LinkedIn, enhancing engagement.
- **LinkedIn Live**: Live streaming feature that allows users to broadcast events, webinars, and other live content to their network in real time.
- **Video Messaging**: Personalized video messages sent directly to connections, offering a more personal touch in communication.

Increased Emphasis on Community and Networking

LinkedIn continues to emphasize the importance of community building and networking:

- **LinkedIn Groups**: Enhanced functionality and discoverability of LinkedIn Groups for niche communities and professional discussions.
- **Events**: Integration of virtual events and webinars, allowing users to host and participate in events directly on the platform.
- **Networking Features**: Tools such as the "Find Nearby" feature facilitate real-time networking opportunities during events and conferences.

Advanced Analytics and Insights

LinkedIn is providing more advanced analytics tools for users to track and measure performance:

- **Content Performance Metrics**: Detailed insights into the performance of posts, articles, and videos, including engagement metrics and audience demographics.
- **Company Page Analytics**: Enhanced analytics for company pages, providing data on visitor demographics, follower growth, and engagement trends.
- **Ad Campaign Analytics**: Comprehensive metrics for LinkedIn ad campaigns, enabling better optimization and ROI tracking.

Focus on Professional Development

LinkedIn Learning and other professional development features are gaining prominence:

- **LinkedIn Learning**: Extensive library of courses and learning paths to help users develop new skills and advance their careers.
- **Skill Assessments**: Tools for users to validate their skills through assessments and showcase their proficiency on their profiles.
- **Career Insights**: Data-driven insights into career paths, job market trends, and salary information to guide users in their professional journeys.

Emphasis on Diversity, Equity, and Inclusion (DEI)

LinkedIn is promoting diversity, equity, and inclusion within its community:

- **Content and Conversations**: Encouraging discussions and content around DEI topics, providing a platform for diverse voices.
- **Company Initiatives**: Highlighting companies that are making strides in DEI and sharing best practices.
- **Inclusive Features**: Introducing features that promote inclusivity, such as name pronunciation guides and expanded gender pronoun options.

Integration with Other Platforms and Tools

LinkedIn is increasingly integrating with other platforms and tools to enhance its functionality:

- **CRM Integrations**: Seamless integration with customer relationship management (CRM) systems to streamline lead generation and management.
- **Third-Party Apps**: Partnerships with third-party apps and tools for enhanced marketing, analytics, and productivity.
- **Cross-Platform Marketing**: Ability to coordinate marketing efforts across LinkedIn and other social media platforms for a cohesive strategy.

The evolving LinkedIn landscape offers marketers numerous opportunities to engage their audience, build meaningful relationships, and drive business growth. By staying attuned to these changes and leveraging new features and tools, businesses can maintain a competitive edge on the platform. Embracing enhanced user experiences, diverse content formats, advanced analytics, professional development opportunities, and a focus on DEI will be essential for thriving in the dynamic LinkedIn environment. In the following sections, we will explore how to implement these trends effectively in your LinkedIn marketing strategy.

8.2 Emerging Technologies and Features

As LinkedIn continues to innovate and evolve, emerging technologies and new features are transforming how businesses and professionals use the platform. This section explores some of the most promising technologies and features that are set to shape the future of LinkedIn marketing.

Artificial Intelligence and Machine Learning

AI and machine learning are becoming integral to LinkedIn's functionality, enhancing user experience and marketing effectiveness:

- **Personalized Content Recommendations**: AI algorithms analyze user behavior and preferences to deliver tailored content suggestions, improving content relevance and engagement.
- **Smart Replies**: AI-driven smart replies offer suggested responses to messages, streamlining communication and saving time.
- **Predictive Analytics**: Machine learning models predict user behavior and content performance, enabling marketers to optimize their strategies and focus on high-potential opportunities.

LinkedIn Live and Enhanced Video Features

Video content is gaining traction on LinkedIn, and new video features are making it more engaging and accessible:

- **LinkedIn Live**: Live streaming allows users to broadcast events, webinars, and Q&A sessions in real time, fostering immediate interaction with their audience.
- **Video Messaging**: Personalized video messages enhance communication, making interactions more engaging and memorable.
- **Advanced Video Analytics**: Enhanced video analytics provide insights into viewer engagement, helping marketers refine their video content strategies.

Augmented Reality (AR) and Virtual Reality (VR)

AR and VR technologies are gradually being integrated into LinkedIn, offering immersive and interactive experiences:

- **Virtual Events and Conferences**: VR enables users to attend virtual events and conferences, creating a more engaging and interactive experience than traditional online events.
- **AR Advertisements**: Interactive AR ads allow users to experience products and services in a more immersive way, increasing engagement and conversion rates.
- **Virtual Networking**: VR technology facilitates virtual networking sessions, making it easier to connect and interact with professionals in a realistic environment.

Advanced Analytics and Reporting Tools

Enhanced analytics and reporting tools provide deeper insights and more actionable data for marketers:

- **Real-Time Analytics**: Access to real-time data allows marketers to make quick adjustments to their campaigns for optimal performance.
- **Attribution Models**: Advanced attribution models help marketers understand the customer journey and the impact of different touchpoints on conversions.
- **Cross-Channel Analytics**: Integration with other marketing platforms enables comprehensive analysis of cross-channel

marketing efforts, providing a holistic view of campaign performance.

Enhanced LinkedIn Learning and Skill Assessments

LinkedIn Learning is continuously expanding its offerings, and new features are making professional development more personalized and impactful:

- **Personalized Learning Paths**: AI-driven recommendations suggest courses and learning paths based on users' career goals and skill gaps.
- **Skill Assessments**: Enhanced skill assessments validate users' proficiencies, allowing them to showcase their verified skills on their profiles.
- **Interactive Learning Experiences**: New interactive features, such as quizzes and hands-on projects, make learning more engaging and effective.

Integration with Other Business Tools

LinkedIn is enhancing its integration with various business tools to streamline workflows and improve productivity:

- **CRM Integrations**: Seamless integration with CRM systems like Salesforce and HubSpot facilitates lead management and nurtures customer relationships.

- **Marketing Automation**: Integration with marketing automation platforms allows for coordinated and efficient campaign management across multiple channels.
- **Collaboration Tools**: Enhanced integration with collaboration tools like Microsoft Teams and Slack supports better team communication and project management.

Blockchain Technology for Enhanced Security

Blockchain technology offers the potential for improved security and trust on LinkedIn:

- **Data Security**: Blockchain can enhance data security by providing a decentralized and tamper-proof system for storing and managing user information.
- **Verified Credentials**: Blockchain can be used to verify educational and professional credentials, ensuring the authenticity of users' profiles and reducing fraud.

Sustainability and Green Technologies

As sustainability becomes a priority, LinkedIn is incorporating green technologies and promoting environmentally responsible practices:

- **Green Advertising**: Eco-friendly advertising options and sustainability-focused content encourage responsible marketing practices.

- **Corporate Social Responsibility (CSR) Integration**: Features that highlight companies' CSR efforts and sustainability initiatives enhance brand reputation and attract socially conscious professionals.
- **Energy-Efficient Data Centers**: LinkedIn's commitment to using energy-efficient data centers reduces its environmental impact and supports sustainability goals.

Emerging technologies and new features are revolutionizing how LinkedIn is used for professional networking, marketing, and business development. AI and machine learning, enhanced video capabilities, AR and VR, advanced analytics, LinkedIn Learning, tool integrations, blockchain technology, and sustainability initiatives are all playing a pivotal role in shaping the future of the platform. By staying informed about these innovations and strategically incorporating them into their LinkedIn marketing strategies, businesses can maintain a competitive edge and maximize their success on the platform. In the next sections, we will delve into practical applications and strategies for leveraging these emerging technologies and features in your LinkedIn marketing efforts.

8.3 Preparing for Changes in LinkedIn Algorithms

Understanding and adapting to changes in LinkedIn algorithms is essential for maintaining and enhancing your marketing effectiveness on the platform. LinkedIn's algorithms determine the visibility of your content, the reach of your posts, and how your profile is ranked in search results. This section explores strategies for preparing and adapting to these algorithm changes to ensure continued success on LinkedIn.

Understanding LinkedIn's Algorithm

LinkedIn's algorithm is designed to prioritize relevant, engaging, and high-quality content. Key factors influencing the algorithm include:

- **Engagement**: Content that receives likes, comments, and shares is prioritized, as it indicates relevance and value.
- **Relevance**: The algorithm assesses the relevance of content to a user's interests, based on their interactions and profile information.
- **Timeliness**: Recent posts are more likely to appear in users' feeds, ensuring that content is timely and up-to-date.
- **Connections**: Content from users' connections and their network is prioritized, fostering engagement within existing networks.
- **Content-Type**: Different types of content (text, video, images, articles) are weighed differently, with a current trend towards favoring video content.

Strategies for Adapting to Algorithm Changes

To stay ahead of algorithm changes and maintain a strong presence on LinkedIn, consider the following strategies:

1. Prioritize High-Quality Content

Creating high-quality, valuable content is essential for algorithm success:

- **Engaging Posts**: Share informative, thought-provoking, and engaging content that encourages likes, comments, and shares.
- **Visual Content**: Use images, infographics, and videos to make your posts visually appealing and more likely to capture attention.
- **Authenticity**: Authentic and relatable content resonates more with audiences, fostering genuine engagement.

2. Encourage and Engage in Conversations

Active engagement with your audience signals to the algorithm that your content is valuable:

- **Prompt Responses**: Respond to comments on your posts promptly to encourage further discussion and engagement.
- **Ask Questions**: Include questions in your posts to stimulate conversation and invite opinions.
- **Engage with Others**: Actively comment on and engage with content from your connections to build relationships and increase your visibility.

3. Optimize Posting Frequency and Timing

Consistency and timing can significantly impact your content's reach:

- **Regular Posting**: Maintain a consistent posting schedule to keep your audience engaged and improve your algorithmic ranking.

- **Optimal Timing**: Post during peak times when your audience is most active, typically during business hours on weekdays.

4. Leverage LinkedIn's Features

Utilize LinkedIn's diverse features to maximize your content's visibility and engagement:

- **LinkedIn Articles**: Publish long-form articles to showcase your expertise and provide in-depth insights.
- **LinkedIn Stories**: Use Stories for short, engaging updates and behind-the-scenes content.
- **LinkedIn Live**: Host live events to engage with your audience in real time and boost visibility.

5. Monitor Analytics and Adjust Strategies

Regularly analyze your LinkedIn performance metrics to understand what works and refine your strategy:

- **Content Performance**: Use LinkedIn's analytics tools to track engagement metrics, such as views, likes, comments, and shares.
- **Audience Insights**: Understand your audience demographics and preferences to tailor your content more effectively.
- **A/B Testing**: Experiment with different types of content, posting times, and formats to see what resonates best with your audience.

Staying Informed About Algorithm Updates

Keeping up-to-date with LinkedIn's algorithm changes ensures you can quickly adapt your strategies:

- **LinkedIn Announcements**: Follow LinkedIn's official blog and updates to stay informed about new features and algorithm changes.
- **Industry News**: Read industry publications and join professional groups to learn about trends and best practices in LinkedIn marketing.
- **Continuous Learning**: Attend webinars, workshops, and training sessions focused on LinkedIn marketing and algorithm updates.

Preparing for changes in LinkedIn algorithms requires a proactive approach, focusing on high-quality content, active engagement, optimized posting strategies, and leveraging platform features. By staying informed and adaptable, you can ensure your LinkedIn marketing efforts remain effective and continue to drive meaningful engagement and conversions. In the subsequent sections, we will explore how to implement these strategies in detail and provide practical tips for maximizing your success on LinkedIn.

8.4 The Role of AI and Automation in LinkedIn Marketing

Artificial Intelligence (AI) and automation are transforming LinkedIn marketing, providing tools and insights that enhance efficiency, effectiveness, and engagement. Leveraging these technologies can help marketers optimize their strategies, personalize interactions, and achieve better results with less effort. This section explores the role of AI and automation in LinkedIn marketing and how to effectively incorporate them into your strategy.

AI in LinkedIn Marketing

AI is revolutionizing how marketers approach LinkedIn, offering powerful capabilities for data analysis, content creation, and audience targeting. Key areas where AI is making a significant impact include:

1. Predictive Analytics

AI-powered predictive analytics can forecast trends and behaviors, enabling marketers to:

- **Identify High-Value Leads**: Predict which leads are most likely to convert based on historical data and user behavior.
- **Optimize Content Strategies**: Determine what types of content will resonate most with your audience and when to post for maximum engagement.
- **Enhance Campaign Performance**: Use predictive models to anticipate campaign outcomes and adjust strategies accordingly.

2. Personalization

AI allows for advanced personalization, creating more relevant and engaging experiences for users:

- **Dynamic Content**: Tailor content and recommendations based on individual user preferences, behavior, and interactions.
- **Customized Messaging**: Use AI to craft personalized messages for different segments of your audience, increasing relevance and response rates.
- **Behavioral Insights**: Analyze user behavior to deliver personalized content and experiences that match their interests and needs.

3. Content Creation and Curation

AI tools can assist in creating and curating content, saving time, and ensuring quality:

- **Automated Writing**: AI-powered writing tools can generate content, such as articles and posts, based on specified topics and keywords.
- **Content Suggestions**: AI can recommend content ideas and topics that are trending and relevant to your audience.
- **Visual Content**: Use AI to create and enhance visual content, such as images and videos, to make your posts more engaging.

Automation in LinkedIn Marketing

Automation streamlines repetitive tasks and processes, allowing marketers to focus on strategy and creative aspects. Key areas where automation can be effectively utilized include:

1. Scheduling and Posting

Automated tools can manage your content calendar and ensure consistent posting:

- **Post Scheduling**: Use automation tools to schedule posts in advance, ensuring a steady stream of content even during off-hours.
- **Content Distribution**: Automatically distribute content across multiple channels and groups to maximize reach and engagement.

2. Lead Generation and Nurturing

Automation can enhance lead generation efforts and nurture relationships with potential clients:

- **Lead Capture**: Use automated forms and chatbots to capture lead information directly from LinkedIn.

- **Email Sequences**: Automate email follow-ups and nurturing sequences to keep leads engaged and move them through the sales funnel.
- **Lead Scoring**: Implement automated lead scoring to prioritize high-value prospects and focus efforts where they are most likely to yield results.

3. Engagement and Interaction

Automation tools can help maintain consistent engagement with your audience:

- **Auto-Responses**: Use AI-powered chatbots to provide instant responses to common inquiries and keep users engaged.
- **Personalized Outreach**: Automate personalized connection requests and messages to expand your network efficiently.
- **Event Invitations**: Automate the process of inviting connections to events and webinars, ensuring no one is missed.

Integrating AI and Automation into Your Strategy

To effectively integrate AI and automation into your LinkedIn marketing strategy, consider the following steps:

1. Identify Key Areas for Automation

Determine which tasks and processes can be automated to save time and increase efficiency. Focus on areas such as content scheduling, lead generation, and engagement.

2. Choose the Right Tools

Select AI and automation tools that align with your marketing goals and integrate well with LinkedIn. Popular tools include Hootsuite for scheduling, LinkedIn Sales Navigator for lead generation, and Drift for chatbots.

3. Monitor and Adjust

Regularly monitor the performance of your AI and automation efforts. Use analytics to assess what's working and make adjustments as needed to optimize results.

4. Balance Automation with Human Touch

While automation can handle many tasks, maintaining a human touch is crucial for building genuine relationships. Ensure that your automated processes still allow for personalized, authentic interactions.

AI and automation are powerful allies in LinkedIn marketing, offering opportunities to enhance efficiency, personalization, and overall effectiveness. By integrating these technologies into your strategy, you can stay ahead of the competition, engage more effectively with your audience, and achieve better marketing outcomes. In the following sections, we will explore practical applications and detailed strategies for leveraging AI and automation on LinkedIn to maximize your marketing success.

8.5 Future Predictions and Strategies for Success

As LinkedIn continues to grow and evolve, staying ahead of future trends and predictions will be crucial for maintaining a competitive edge in your marketing efforts. This section explores key predictions for the future of LinkedIn marketing and offers strategies to ensure continued success on the platform.

Future Predictions

1. Increased Focus on Video Content

Video content is set to become even more dominant on LinkedIn:

- **Live Streaming Growth**: LinkedIn Live will become a staple for brands, with more companies using live streams for events, product launches, and real-time engagement.
- **Short-Form Video**: Similar to TikTok and Instagram Reels, LinkedIn may introduce short-form video formats to cater to quick, digestible content preferences.

2. Enhanced AI and Machine Learning Integration

AI and machine learning will play an even bigger role in LinkedIn's functionalities:

- **Smarter Algorithms**: Improved algorithms will offer more personalized content and better matching for job seekers and employers.
- **Advanced Analytics**: AI will provide deeper insights and predictive analytics, helping marketers make more informed decisions.

3. Expansion of E-Commerce Capabilities

LinkedIn may introduce more e-commerce features, integrating direct sales opportunities:

- **Shoppable Posts**: Posts and ads may become directly shoppable, allowing users to purchase products without leaving the platform.
- **Enhanced Business Pages**: Company pages might offer integrated storefronts, making it easier for businesses to showcase and sell products directly on LinkedIn.

4. Greater Emphasis on Thought Leadership and Expertise

Building authority and credibility will continue to be crucial:

- **Content Hubs**: LinkedIn may develop dedicated spaces for industry experts to share insights, conduct discussions, and build communities.
- **Professional Certifications**: Enhanced focus on LinkedIn Learning and certifications to validate skills and expertise.

5. Increased Use of Automation Tools

Automation will become more sophisticated and widespread:

- **Advanced CRM Integrations**: Deeper integration with CRM systems to streamline lead management and nurturing.
- **Automated Content Creation**: AI-driven tools will assist in creating high-quality content, including text, images, and videos.

Strategies for Future Success

1. Embrace Video and Live Content

Incorporate more video content into your LinkedIn strategy:

- **Regular Live Streams**: Host regular live events to engage with your audience in real time. Use LinkedIn Live for product launches, Q&A sessions, and industry discussions.
- **Professional Videos**: Invest in high-quality video production for tutorials, case studies, and behind-the-scenes content.

2. Leverage AI and Automation

Utilize AI and automation tools to enhance your marketing efforts:

- **Predictive Analytics**: Use AI-driven analytics to anticipate trends and tailor your content strategy accordingly.
- **Chatbots**: Implement AI chatbots to handle customer inquiries, providing instant responses and improving user experience.
- **Automated Personalization**: Use automation to deliver personalized content and messages at scale, ensuring relevance and engagement.

3. Focus on Thought Leadership

Position yourself and your brand as industry leaders:

- **Publish Articles**: Regularly publish in-depth articles and insights on LinkedIn to showcase your expertise.
- **Engage in Discussions**: Participate in LinkedIn Groups and industry discussions to build your reputation and connect with other thought leaders.
- **Offer Webinars**: Host webinars and online workshops to share knowledge and engage with your audience.

4. Optimize for E-Commerce

Prepare for potential e-commerce integrations on LinkedIn:

- **Shoppable Content**: Create content that highlights your products and services, making it easy for users to learn more and make purchases.
- **Enhanced Company Pages**: Ensure your company page is optimized with detailed product information, customer testimonials, and clear calls to action.

5. Stay Agile and Adaptable

Be ready to adapt to new trends and changes:

- **Continuous Learning**: Keep up-to-date with LinkedIn's updates and industry trends through professional development and networking.
- **Experimentation**: Regularly test new features and strategies to see what works best for your audience.
- **Feedback Loops**: Use feedback from your audience to refine your approach and stay aligned with their needs and preferences.

The future of LinkedIn marketing promises exciting developments in video content, AI integration, e-commerce capabilities, thought leadership, and automation. By embracing these trends and implementing forward-thinking strategies, you can ensure your marketing efforts remain effective and impactful. Staying agile, continuously learning, and adapting to new features will be key to maintaining a competitive edge and achieving sustained success on LinkedIn. In the final sections of this book, we will recap the essential takeaways and provide a comprehensive roadmap for implementing the strategies discussed throughout.

Conclusion

"LinkedIn Marketing 2024: A Comprehensive Guide to Successful Marketing, Engagement, and Conversions with Proven Tactics, Techniques, and Strategies on the World's Largest Professional Networking Platform" has taken you through the intricate and dynamic landscape of LinkedIn marketing. From the foundational elements of setting up professional profiles and company pages to the advanced tactics of leveraging AI, automation, and emerging technologies, this guide aims to equip you with the knowledge and tools necessary to excel on LinkedIn.

The Journey through LinkedIn Marketing

We began our journey by understanding LinkedIn as a powerful marketing platform. Recognizing its unique role in both B2B and B2C contexts, we explored the importance of crafting professional profiles and compelling company pages. These initial steps lay the groundwork for a successful presence on LinkedIn, ensuring that both individuals and companies can present themselves effectively to their target audience.

Building and Optimizing Your Network

The next phase focused on building and optimizing your LinkedIn network. Identifying your target audience, growing your professional connections, and leveraging LinkedIn Groups were key strategies discussed. Establishing strong connections and nurturing relationships are crucial for expanding your reach and influence on the platform.

Content Marketing Mastery

Content marketing on LinkedIn was addressed in-depth, highlighting the importance of a well-developed content strategy. From creating engaging posts and articles to utilizing LinkedIn videos for maximum impact, we covered various content types that resonate best with LinkedIn's professional audience. Developing a robust content plan and consistently delivering value to your network is essential for maintaining engagement and driving conversions.

Leveraging LinkedIn Advertising

We explored LinkedIn advertising strategies, providing insights into understanding different ad formats, setting up and managing ads, and targeting options. Creating compelling ad creatives and analyzing ad performance are critical components of a successful LinkedIn advertising campaign. These strategies help ensure that your marketing efforts are not only seen but also acted upon by your desired audience.

Analytics and Optimization

Understanding and utilizing LinkedIn analytics was another significant focus. By measuring key metrics and KPIs, and using analytics to refine your strategy, you can continuously improve your marketing efforts. Reporting and presenting your results effectively helps in demonstrating the value of your LinkedIn activities and securing buy-in from stakeholders.

Advanced Tactics and Future Trends

We delved into advanced LinkedIn marketing tactics, such as using LinkedIn Sales Navigator for lead generation, implementing InMail campaigns, and leveraging events and webinars. Collaborations and influencer marketing were also discussed as powerful strategies for amplifying your reach. Looking ahead, we explored future trends and innovations, including the role of AI, automation, and emerging technologies.

Preparing for the Future

The final chapters addressed preparing for changes in LinkedIn algorithms and the increasing role of AI and automation. Staying informed and adaptable to these changes will be crucial for maintaining a competitive edge. We also discussed future predictions and strategies for success, emphasizing the importance of video content, thought leadership, and optimizing for potential e-commerce capabilities.

A Roadmap to Success

As we conclude, it's important to synthesize these insights into a cohesive roadmap for success. Start by establishing a strong foundation with professional profiles and company pages. Build and nurture your network, consistently deliver high-quality content, and leverage advertising and analytics to optimize your efforts. Stay informed about emerging trends and be ready to adapt your strategies as LinkedIn continues to evolve.

Final Thoughts

LinkedIn offers unparalleled opportunities for professional networking, marketing, and business growth. By applying the proven tactics, techniques, and strategies outlined in this guide, you can harness the full potential of the platform. Whether you're looking to build brand awareness, generate leads, or drive conversions, LinkedIn provides the tools and audience to achieve your goals.

Thank you for embarking on this journey through LinkedIn marketing. With dedication, creativity, and strategic thinking, you can turn LinkedIn into a powerful asset for your marketing efforts in 2024 and beyond. Here's to your continued success on the world's largest professional networking platform.

www.ingramcontent.com/pod-product-compliance
Lightning Source LLC
LaVergne TN
LVHW081521050326
832903LV00025B/1570